Teaching the Annotated Bibliography

This book informs instructors and librarians about the history, aims, and pedagogical uses of the annotated bibliography.

A companion to the authors' *Writing the Annotated Bibliography*, this text enables instructors to better understand the annotated bibliography not only as a tool for research and composition but also as a valuable pedagogical tool. It provides practical guidance along with assignments, lesson plans, assessment rubrics, and other tools for using annotated bibliographies in effective and nuanced ways. It also contains annotated bibliography samples in APA, MLA, and Chicago styles.

This practical book is of great use to instructors of composition and research skills, librarians, curriculum designers, writing center directors, and education professionals.

Cynthia A. Cochran is an Associate Professor of English at Illinois College, USA. She is a writing studies expert with 30 years of experience directing writing centers and working with writing across the curriculum and writing programs. Cindy has an MS in Education from the University of Illinois and a PhD in English from Carnegie Mellon University.

Luke Beatty is a Library Director and an Associate Professor of Library Science at St. Ambrose University, USA. He has worked in academic libraries for over a decade. Luke has an MLIS and an MEd from the University of Western Ontario.

Teaching the Annotated Bibliography
A Resource for Instructors, Librarians, and Other Academic Professionals

Cynthia A. Cochran and Luke Beatty

NEW YORK AND LONDON

First published 2023
by Routledge
605 Third Avenue, New York, NY 10158

and by Routledge
4 Park Square, Milton Park, Abingdon, Oxon, OX14 4RN

Routledge is an imprint of the Taylor & Francis Group, an informa business

© 2023 Cynthia A. Cochran and Luke Beatty

The right of Cynthia A. Cochran and Luke Beatty to be identified as authors of this work has been asserted in accordance with sections 77 and 78 of the Copyright, Designs and Patents Act 1988.

All rights reserved. No part of this book may be reprinted or reproduced or utilised in any form or by any electronic, mechanical, or other means, now known or hereafter invented, including photocopying and recording, or in any information storage or retrieval system, without permission in writing from the publishers.

Trademark notice: Product or corporate names may be trademarks or registered trademarks, and are used only for identification and explanation without intent to infringe.

Library of Congress Cataloging-in-Publication Data
Names: Cochran, Cynthia A., author. | Beatty, Luke, author.
Title: Teaching the annotated bibliography: a resource for instructors, librarians, and other academic professionals / by Cynthia A. Cochran & Luke Beatty.
Description: New York: Routledge, 2022. | Includes bibliographical references and index. | Identifiers: LCCN 2022020436 (print) | LCCN 2022020437 (ebook) | ISBN 9781032077451 (hardback) | ISBN 9781032102580 (paperback) | ISBN 9781003214434 (ebook)
Subjects: LCSH: Bibliography—Study and teaching (Higher)
Classification: LCC Z1001.C63 2022 (print) |
LCC Z1001 (ebook) | DDC 010.71/1—dc23/eng/20220520
LC record available at https://lccn.loc.gov/2022020436
LC ebook record available at https://lccn.loc.gov/2022020437

ISBN: 978-1-032-07745-1 (hbk)
ISBN: 978-1-032-10258-0 (pbk)
ISBN: 978-1-003-21443-4 (ebk)

DOI: 10.4324/9781003214434

Typeset in Times New Roman
by codeMantra

Cindy Cochran
- To Bob: thank you for all your support, love, and patience.
- To my family and friends: thank you for letting me ignore you while I wrote this book.
- To Claudia McCabe, Bonnie Seebold, Roland Holmes, Rand Spiro, Nancy Nelson Spivey, Dick Hayes, and Richard L. Enos: thank you for inspiring me.
- To Luke: thank you for your great ideas, organizational prowess, weird humor, and candy drawer.
- To my pets: thank you for being furry and funny.

Luke Beatty
- To my family and friends: thank you for everything.
- To my pets: thank you for being wonderful companions.
- To Cindy Cochran: thank you for writing this book with me.
- To Graham Parker, King's X, The Sea and Cake, and Vince Guaraldi: thank you for providing the soundtrack to this book.

Contents

Acknowledgments   xiii
Preface   xv

1 History of the Annotated Bibliography   1
CYNTHIA A. COCHRAN

Introduction 1
Annotations 1
Citations 2
Bibliographies 3
Annotated Bibliographies 4
Related Forms 5
Annotated Bibliography and Related Forms Online 5

2 The Annotated Bibliography in Higher Education   9
LUKE BEATTY

Introduction 9
Manuals and Skill Books 10
Librarian and Instructor Collaboration 11
First-Year Writing and General Education Courses 14
Humanities and Social Sciences 15
Hard Sciences 17
Scaffolding 18
Student Learning and Assessment 19
Online and Web 21

3 Teaching Annotation Types   24
CYNTHIA A. COCHRAN AND LUKE BEATTY

Annotation Types 24
Descriptive Annotations 26

Descriptive Annotation Example in MLA 9   26
Descriptive Annotation Checklist   27
Descriptive Annotation Checklist   28
Summative Annotations   29
Summative Annotation Example in MLA 9   29
Summative Annotation Checklist   31
Summative Annotation Checklist   31
Evaluative Annotations   32
Evaluative Annotation Example in MLA 9   32
Evaluative Annotation Checklist   34
Evaluative Annotation Checklist   34
Reflective Annotations   35
Reflective Annotation Example in MLA 9   35
Reflective Annotation Checklist   37
Reflective Annotation Checklist   37
Combined Annotations   38
Combined Annotation Example in MLA 9   39
Combined Annotation Checklist   39
Combined Annotation Checklist   40

4 Assignments for Composition and WAC Classes   42
CYNTHIA A. COCHRAN

Introduction   42
Preliminary Notes on Instruction   44
Assignment #1: Basic Annotation Skills   46
   Audience   46
   Timeline   46
   Learning Outcomes / Students Will...   46
   Activity Description   46
   Teaching Notes   47
   Variants   48
Basic Annotation Skills Instructions   49
   Basic Annotation Skills Rubric   51
Assignment #2: Preliminary Annotated Bibliography   53
   Audience   53
   Timeline   53
   Learning Outcomes / Students Will...   53
   Activity Description   53
   Teaching Notes   54
   Variants   55
Preliminary Annotated Bibliography Instructions   56

Preliminary Annotated Bibliography Rubric 58
Assignment #3: Complete Annotated Bibliography 60
   Audience 60
   Timeline 60
   Learning Outcomes / Students Will... 60
   Activity Description 61
   Teaching Notes 61
   Variants 63
   Complete Annotated Bibliography Instructions 64
   Complete Annotated Bibliography Rubric 66
Assignment #4: Annotated Bibliography and
  Argumentative Essay 69
   Audience 69
   Timeline 69
   Learning Outcomes / Students Will... 69
   Activity Description 70
   Teaching Notes 70
   Variants 72
Annotated Bibliography and Argumentative Essay
  Instructions 73
   Annotated Bibliography and Argumentative Essay
   Rubric 75
Assignment #5: Bibliographic Essay 77
   Audience 77
   Timeline 77
   Learning Outcomes / Students Will... 77
   Activity Description 78
   Teaching Notes 78
   Variants 80
Annotated Bibliography with Bibliographic Essay
  Instructions 81
Annotated Bibliography with Bibliographic Essay
  Rubric 83
Assignment #6: Collaborative Annotated Bibliography 85
   Audience 85
   Timeline 85
   Learning Outcomes / Students Will... 85
   Activity Description 86
   Teaching Notes 86
   Variants 88
Collaborative Annotated Bibliography Instructions 89
   Collaborative Annotated Bibliography Rubric 90

5 Librarian Assignments 93
LUKE BEATTY

Introduction 93
Common Elements – Information Literacy Instruction 94
Common Elements – Citation 94
Common Elements – Formatting 95
Common Elements – Assignment Design 95
Common Elements – Assignment Sheet 96
  Baseline Annotated Bibliography Assignment Sheet 97
Assignment #1: The Simplest Annotated Bibliography 99
  Outcomes / Students Will… 99
  Standards Alignment 100
  Baseline Assignment Sheet Changes 100
  Teaching Notes 100
  Suggested Rubric 101
  Further Reading 102
Assignment #2: Annotated Bibliography with Different Source Types 103
  Outcomes / Students Will… 103
  Standards Alignment 104
  Baseline Assignment Sheet Changes 104
  Teaching Notes 105
  Suggested Rubric 106
  Further Reading 107
Assignment #3: Annotated Bibliography with Combined Annotations 108
  Outcomes / Students Will… 108
  Standards Alignment 109
  Baseline Assignment Sheet Changes 109
  Teaching Notes 110
  Suggested Rubric 111
  Further Reading 113
Assignment #4: Source Evaluation Annotated Bibliography 114
  Outcomes / Students Will… 114
  Standards Alignment 115
  Baseline Assignment Sheet Changes 116
  Teaching Notes 116
  Suggested Rubric 116
  Further Reading 117
Assignment #5: Visual Annotated Bibliography 118

Outcomes / Students Will... 118
Standards Alignment 119
Baseline Assignment Sheet Changes 119
Teaching Notes 120
Suggested Rubric 120
Further Reading 121
Assignment #6: Group Annotated Bibliography 122
Outcomes / Students Will... 122
Standards Alignment 123
Baseline Assignment Sheet Changes 123
Teaching Notes 124
Suggested Rubric 125
Further Reading 126
Assignment #7: Scaffolded Annotated Bibliography 127
Outcomes / Students Will... 127
Standards Alignment 128
Baseline Assignment Sheet Changes 128
Teaching Notes 129
Suggested Rubric 130
Further Reading 131

6 Library Support 138
LUKE BEATTY

Introduction 138
Single-Session Support 138
Reference Desk Work 139
Production of Educational Materials 140
Faculty Liaison and Outreach 141
Collaboration with Other Campus Offices 142

7 Writing Center and Academic Coaching Support 144
CYNTHIA A. COCHRAN

Introduction 144
Beginning the Support Session 144
Checking Annotated Bibliography Format 145
Annotated Bibliography: [My Topic] 146
Introductory Paragraphs 147
Annotation Entries 147
Concluding Paragraphs 148
Checking Documentation Format 148

Contents

    Helping with Annotations 150
    CHECKLIST: Things to Consider for a Complete
      Combined Annotation 152
    Significant Problems to Consider 153

8 Teaching Source Types   155
LUKE BEATTY AND CYNTHIA A. COCHRAN

    Introduction 155
    Books 156
    Book Chapters/Book Sections 156
    Academic Journal Articles 157
    Encyclopedia Articles 158
    Magazine Articles 159
    Newspaper Articles 159
    Websites and Webpages 160
    Blogs, Podcasts, and Social Media 161
    Audiovisual Material 161
    Government Publications and Technical Reports 162
    Images and Art 163
    Dissertations and Theses 163
    Videogames 164
    Literary Works 165

9 Three Sample Annotated Bibliographies   166
LUKE BEATTY AND CYNTHIA A. COCHRAN

    Introduction 166
    Sample APA 7 Annotated Bibliography 166
    Sample MLA 9 Annotated Bibliography 170
    Sample Chicago 17 (Notes and Bibliography)
      Annotated Bibliography 173

Glossary   177
Index   179

Acknowledgments

Cindy would like to acknowledge Brian and all the folks at Routledge, who have been so supportive in getting this book to press. Thanks to Kacie Wills for introducing me to *Omeka*, and the rest of the Illinois College English Department for their teaching ideas. Thanks to Michael Michaud for his creativity in writing about writing. Thanks to the Central Illinois Philosophy Group for their astute commentary on an early version of Chapter #1. And thanks to students in my composition courses, who have tested several versions of annotated bibliography assignments and rubrics.

Luke would like to acknowledge the following folks for helping get this book to the finish line:

- My erstwhile colleagues at Schewe Library and our delightfully askew student workers. Thank you for making Schewe Library the wonderful place it is.
- My new colleagues at St. Ambrose University Library. You've all been great. Thank you so much.
- Paul Tarc. For mentoring me back in the day. I wouldn't be here without you. Respect!
- Brian, Grant, Caroline, Sean, and Rajamalar at Routledge. You're a fantastic editorial team, and I appreciate all your work over the last year.

Preface

Welcome to our book! We are Cindy Cochran, Associate Professor of English at Illinois College with over 30 years of teaching experience, and Luke Beatty, Library Director at St. Ambrose University, who has worked in academic libraries for over a decade. Together we have co-taught classes, presented at conferences, and co-authored two books. We're pleased you've come across this book, and we hope you find it worth your time.

For those considering a purchase, know that the book is a quick read; has something for instructors, librarians, writing center staff, and academic coaches; and contains practical advice and useable assignment templates, rubrics, samples, and checklists. Having worked with a variety of annotated bibliography (AB) assignments over the years and having authored *Writing the Annotated Bibliography: A Guide for Students and Researchers*, we think we're the ideal folks to bring an AB book to you.

What will you find in this book?

In the first three chapters, we overview the AB. "Chapter #1: History of the Annotated Bibliography" outlines the history of the AB. "Chapter #2: The Annotated Bibliography in Higher Education" is a thematically organized bibliography about the AB's use in higher education. "Chapter #3: Teaching Annotation Types" concisely overviews the AB and defines the five most common annotation types (descriptive, summative, evaluative, reflective, and combined). For those unfamiliar with teaching ABs, Chapter #3 will be helpful.

The next two chapters contain a variety of assignments, rubrics, and teaching advice for instructors and librarians working with ABs. "Chapter #4: Assignments for Composition and WAC Classes" features assignments for composition and writing across the curriculum (WAC) courses. Some of the assignments in this chapter are appropriate for developmental or first-year composition courses; others are suitable for advanced composition classes. Almost all can be adapted to WAC courses at the undergraduate or graduate levels. "Chapter #5: Librarian Assignments" provides seven assignments for librarians teaching (or co-teaching) credit-bearing information literacy courses. Though naturally the two chapters overlap, we assume that instructional faculty will gravitate to Chapter #4 and librarians will use Chapter #5. Feel free to use any materials from these chapters for non-commercial, educational purposes.

The next chapters offer strategies for supporting the AB outside of credit-bearing classrooms. "Chapter #6: Library Support" discusses outside-the-classroom AB support strategies for librarians, while "Chapter #7: Writing Center and Academic Coaching Support" provides strategies for writing centers and academic coaching staff to help students write their ABs. The tips in these chapters are mostly derived from Luke and Cindy's experience working individually with students.

Our final two chapters tie up loose ends. "Chapter #8: Teaching Source Types" sorts through the many types of sources students use in their ABs and discusses how students might best annotate these materials. Finally, "Chapter #9: Three Sample Annotated Bibliographies" models three ABs in the APA 7, MLA 9, and Chicago 17 styles that you can use for educational, non-commercial purposes.

And that's our book. We hope you will find some new ideas for your AB assignments and AB support. Take care!

1 History of the Annotated Bibliography

Cynthia A. Cochran

Introduction

The annotated bibliography (AB) of today has developed out of the history of annotations, citations, and bibliographies, and it is still changing. This chapter contextualizes the AB by discussing historical and recent developments with the form and its constituent parts.

A bit of background: An AB is an ordered list of source citations and notes, or annotations. When annotations are produced as organized notes on sources about a common topic and accompanied by citations, the result is an AB. The five forms of annotations discussed in this book (descriptive, summative, evaluative, reflective, and combined) are commonly used in research.

This chapter argues that annotations, citations, bibliographies, and ABs have all transformed over the years and have spawned related forms, such as bibliographic essays, collaboratively annotated texts, and digital archives.

Annotations

Annotations are generally verbal notes, but can be doodles, complex drawings, or symbols commenting on, adding to, or correcting textual and sometimes non-textual artifacts. They may appear in any margin of a page or be written as a separate document, individually (e.g., on notecards) or grouped (e.g., in an AB). They may be private, shared in a limited way, or public (Agosti and Ferro 3). Before the advent of the printing press, annotations – marginalia including elaborate drawings, doodles, words, and symbols – were commonly added to pages of handwritten and block-printed manuscripts. Thus, books were, in a sense, improved upon by scribes and readers, who chose their placement on the page. After the printing press, many books were published complete with footnotes and marginal annotations relegated to particular positions on the page. Agosti and Ferro say that annotations provide "not only a way of explaining and enriching an information resource with personal observations, but also a means of transmitting and sharing ideas to improve collaborative work practices" (3). Annotations have also functioned as mechanisms to exercise authority, create community consensus, or foster debate (Tribble 14–17). Kalir and Garcia agree that annotations serve to share ideas, initiate debate, and claim power, adding that they also aid in learning while providing information for everyday use (9).

Citations

Citations emerged historically as a way to exchange information about materials owned in private and religious libraries. Early citations were inconsistent in format but usually named authors and titles. Like annotations, early citations tended to be placed in text margins. By the 17th century, scholars typically used "... complex full-cite, letter-and-number systems that used Latin terms" (Connors 11). Connors, in describing the persuasive power of citation systems, credits Edward Gibbon's *The History of the Decline and Fall of the Roman Empire* (1776–1787) as the first volume in which citations became a consistent "literary form" specifying author, title, volume, place of publication, and section or page (35–36).

Before the 1800s, most scholarship had a generally educated audience, but by the 1900s, professions had grown and scholars were narrowing their focus; so scholars, publishers, and editors systemized citation formats. Thus, citations became somewhat more standardized (Connors 39, 42). However, differing citation systems evolved in response to professionals' varied needs and the types of sources they used.

Several citation systems emerged in the 19th and 20th centuries as scholarship proliferated. For example, the US Geological Service and the US Government Printing Office developed style guides in the 1890s (Connors 43). The Harvard style was developed by Edward Laurens Mark, who probably modeled it on the Library of Harvard's Museum of Comparative Zoology system for cataloging artifacts (Chernin 1062–63). These and many other citation styles were naturally inconsistent with one another.

Today, the world has hundreds of citation styles. In-text citations, numbered footnotes and endnotes, and reference lists provide bibliographic information such as author/creator names, titles, publishers, and publication years, and perhaps other elements such as edition numbers. Many citations now include a source's virtual location (i.e., URL, DOI, or database), linking to the source text and creating a hypertext.

The styles most frequently used in the US are those designed by the American Psychological Association (APA), the Modern Languages Association (MLA), and the University of Chicago (Chicago). The APA style, produced in 1929, became the official style of the APA in 1952 as the *APA Publication Manual*. It is commonly used by social science researchers, especially in psychology, education, sociology, and writing studies. This form uses author-date for in-text citations, mainly because of the cumulative nature of scholarship in those fields. The MLA style, popular in the humanities, is taught in many high schools and colleges. The MLA first released its guidelines in 1951 as the *MLA Style Sheet*; after several title changes, it is now known as the *MLA Handbook*. The Chicago style is favored in history, philosophy, religion, and art history. *The Chicago Manual of Style* has been used in various editions since it was first published in 1906 by The University of Chicago Press.

Among other common documentation/citation styles are the American Chemical Society style; the American Medical Association style; the American Sociological Association style; Bluebook (for legal writing); the Council of Science Editors style; the Harvard style (used by many British and Commonwealth researchers); the Electrical and Electronics Engineers style (used in engineering and computer science); and the Oxford style (common in Australia and UK universities).

Bibliographies

Bibliographies first emerged in Egypt. The most famous of these early bibliographies was the *Pinakes*, a listing of classical literature held at the library of Alexandria in the 4th century BCE (Krummel "Bibliography" 522). In the 2nd century, physician Galen made a power-play by publishing an organized list of his own works and denouncing works falsely attributed to him (Balsamo 7). Well before the printing press, there were many informal listings of library holdings and bibliographies of ecclesiastical texts (Krummel "Bibliography" 522–23). For example, the Catholic Church created lists of religious scholarship. In 987/988 CE, in Baghdad, Muhammad ibn Abi Ya'qub Ishaq al-Nadim indexed thousands of authors and works in the *Fihrist al-'Ulum*, including works collected in libraries owned by caliphs, emirs, and other wealthy individuals (Krummel "Bibliography" 522; Wellisch 5, 14). As a term, "bibliography" entered the English-language vocabulary in the second half of the 17th century and, by the 19th century, was known to scholars and booksellers (Balsamo 3).

Once the printing press increased publishing, access to written works, literacy, and scholarship, four types of bibliographies arose: commercial book trade lists (precursors to modern-day book catalogs), topical lists (subject bibliographies), advisory lists of prohibited or recommended materials, and catalogs of library, religious, and private collections (Krummel, "Bibliography" 523).

Annotated Bibliographies

The AB emerged as a way to tell people about library holdings. The academic AB author – whether a librarian or another disciplinary scholar – "gives shape to a diverse (often amorphous) body of scholarly production by classifying, organizing, and evaluating it," so AB authors should have intimate knowledge of their subjects (Colaianne 324).

ABs are published as books, articles, technical reports, and webpages. Some journals, for example, publish occasional or annual ABs on research in a given field, such as that published each November by the *Journal of Research in the Teaching of English*. There are even bibliographies of bibliographies, such as Theodore Besterman's *World Bibliography of Bibliographies*. Published ABs help disciplinary scholars by providing citations, annotations, and author commentary on a given topic. ABs can be organized alphabetically, chronologically, topically, by source format, by language, geographically, by holder (such as museum collections), and by methodology.

The published AB has a long tradition in history, education, library science, communication and rhetoric, literature, and writing studies. It is gaining popularity in other academic areas as well, such as psychology, sociology, and business. With that said, the AB is less commonly used in the physical and biological sciences than in the arts, humanities, and social sciences.

Related Forms

One close relative of the AB is the bibliographic essay, which is particularly prominent in the humanities. Distinguishing the bibliographic essay from the AB is its running commentary on the state of research on a given topic, so that it reads almost like a traditional essay. Typically, a bibliographic essay is organized thematically, and then chronologically, topically, or by author. Some bibliographic essays are book-length.

Another AB-related form is the subject bibliography. Like most library catalogs, subject bibliographies (which are typically ABs-in-disguise) are available online (Krummel "Bibliography" 526). Some subject bibliographies appear on professional organizations' websites.

Annotated Bibliography and Related Forms Online

Online ABs and related forms are often created collaboratively, especially since tools such as *Microsoft Word* and *Google Docs* have greatly eased the process of writing together. For individuals and groups looking to create and publish their ABs, a number of citation management tools are freely available online. See https://library.ic.edu/cite for examples.

A relative of the online AB, the online archival collection, is trending in the digital humanities. Online archival collections of items such as images, texts, and moving pictures are now displayed and accessible on many hosting platforms. Digital archives specialize in giving people virtual access to physical objects (e.g., artworks, scanned texts, antique furniture, coins) and born-digital objects (e.g., online articles, blogs, images). *Drupal* and *Omeka* are two of the most popular content management systems in the digital humanities (Dombrowski 290–92). They allow users to add descriptive and annotative information to items they hold.

For individual users and groups, some common tools for archiving collections include *Diigo Web Collector* (https://www.diigo.com/); *EndNote* (https://endnote.com/); *Evernote* (https://evernote.com/); *Mendeley* (https://www.mendeley.com); *Omeka* (https://endnote.com/); *PowerNotes* (https://powernotes.com/); and *Zotero* (https://

www.zotero.org/). We expect that in the future many more such tools and developments will further alter the AB landscape.

Works Cited

Agosti, Maristella, and Nicola Ferro. "A Formal Model of Annotations of Digital Content." *ACM Transactions on Information Systems*, vol. 26, no. 1, 2007, pp. 3:1–3:57, https://doi.org/10.1145/1292591.1292594.
Balsamo, Luigi. *Bibliography: History of a Tradition*. B.M. Rosenthal, 1990.
Chernin, Eli. "The 'Harvard System': A Mystery Dispelled." *British Medical Journal*, vol. 297, no. 6655, 1988, pp. 1062–63.
Colaianne, A. J. "The Aims and Methods of Annotated Bibliography." *Scholarly Publishing*, vol. 11, no. 4, 1980, pp. 321–31.
Connors, Robert J. "The Rhetoric of Citation Systems, Part I: The Development of Annotation Structures from the Renaissance to 1900." *Rhetoric Review*, vol. 17, no. 1, 1998, pp. 6–48, https://doi.org/10.1080/07350199809359230.
Dombrowski, Quinn. "Drupal and Other Content Management Systems." *Doing Digital Humanities: Practice, Training, Research*, edited by Constance Crompton et al., Routledge, 2016, pp. 289–302, https://doi.org/10.4324/9781315707860.
Kalir, Remi, and Antero Garcia. *Annotation*. The MIT Press, 2021.
Krummel, Donald William. "Bibliography." *Encyclopedia of Library and Information Sciences*, edited by Marcia J. Bates and Mary Niles Maack, 3rd ed., CRC Press, 2011, pp. 522–33, http://dx.doi.org/10.1081/E-ELIS3-120044335.
Tribble, Evelyn B. *Margins and Marginality: The Printed Page in Early Modern England*. University Press of Virginia, 1993.
Wellisch, Hans H. *The First Arab Bibliography: Fihrist al-'Ulum*. University of Illinois Graduate School of Library and Information Science, 1986.

Further Reading

Agosti, Maristella, et al. "A Historical and Contemporary Study on Annotations to Derive Key Features for Systems Design." *International Journal on Digital Libraries*, vol. 8, no. 1, 2007, pp. 1–19, https://doi.org/10.1007/s00799-007-0010-0.
American Psychological Association, editor. *Publication Manual of the American Psychological Association*. 7th ed., American Psychological Association, 2020, https://doi.org/10.1037/0000165-000.
Berger, Sidney E. "Annotations." *The Design of Bibliographies: Observations, References, and Examples*, Greenwood Press, 1992, pp. 35–36.

History of the Annotated Bibliography 7

Bibliography Committee, Collection Development and Evaluation Service. "Guidelines for the Preparation of a Bibliography." *Reference & User Services Quarterly*, vol. 50, no. 1, 2010, pp. 99–101, https://doi.org/10.5860/rusq.50n1.99.

Burkle-Young, Francis A., and Saundra Maley. *The Art of the Footnote[1]: The Intelligent Student's Guide to the Art and Science of Annotating Texts.* University Press of America, 1996.

Connors, Robert J. "The Rhetoric of Citation Systems - Part II: Competing Epistemic Values in Citation." *Rhetoric Review*, vol. 17, no. 2, 1999, pp. 219–45, https://doi.org/10.1080/07350199909359242.

Feather, John. "Bibliography." *International Encyclopedia of Information and Library Science*, edited by John Feather and Paul Sturges, 2nd ed., 2003, pp. 37–38, https://doi.org/10.4324/9780203403303.

Grafton, Anthony. "The Death of the Footnote (Report on an Exaggeration)." *The Wilson Quarterly*, vol. 21, no. 1, 1997, pp. 72–77.

Hackman, Martha L. *The Practical Bibliographer*. Prentice-Hall, 1970.

Harmon, Robert B. "The Dimensions of Bibliography." *Elements of Bibliography: A Guide to Information Sources and Practical Applications*, 3rd ed., Scarecrow Press, 1998, pp. 1–21.

Hauptman, Robert. "Marginalia." *Documentation: A History and Critique of Attribution, Commentary, Glosses, Marginalia, Notes, Bibliographies, Works-Cited Lists, and Citation Indexing and Analysis*, McFarland, 2008, pp. 71–111.

Hemminger, Bradley M., and Julia TerMaat. "Annotating for the World: Attitudes toward Sharing Scholarly Annotations." *Journal of the Association for Information Science and Technology*, vol. 65, no. 11, 2014, pp. 2278–92, https://doi.org/10.1002/asi.23124.

Kalir, Jeremiah H., and Jeremy Dean. "Web Annotation as Conversation and Interruption." *Media Practice and Education*, vol. 19, no. 1, 2018, pp. 18–29, https://doi.org/10.1080/14682753.2017.1362168.

Krummel, Donald William. "Annotation." *Bibliographies: Their Aims and Methods*, H.W. Wilson Co., 1984, pp. 75–84.

Menapace, John. "Some Approaches to Annotation." *Scholarly Publishing*, vol. 1, no. 2, 1970, pp. 194–205.

Modern Language Association of America, editor. *MLA Handbook*. 9th ed., The Modern Language Association of America, 2021.

Nicholas, Rosslyn M., et al. *Basic Bibliography Book: A Brief Guide to Compiling Bibliographies*. Elm Publications, 1984.

Robinson, Antony Meredith Lewin, and Margaret Lodder. "The Meaning of Bibliography and Its Varied Forms." *Systematic Bibliography: A Practical Guide to the Work of Compilation*, 4th ed., Clive Bingley, 1979, pp. 7–17.

Sanders, Erhard. "Indexing an Annotated Bibliography: Step-by-Step Procedure." *Special Libraries*, vol. 64, no. 2, 1973, pp. 87–90.

Savage, Ernest A., and Ernest A. Baker. *Manual of Descriptive Annotation for Library Catalogues*. Library Supply Company, 1906.

Singerman, Robert. "Compiling the Book-length Bibliography: Concepts and Strategies." *Judaica Librarianship*, vol. 2, no. 1/2, 1985, pp. 79–80.

Staines, Heather Ruland. "Digital Open Annotation with Hypothesis: Supplying the Missing Capability of the Web." *Journal of Scholarly Publishing*, vol. 49, no. 3, 2018, pp. 345–65, https://doi.org/10.3138/jsp.49.3.04.

Tanselle, G. Thomas. "Issues in Bibliographical Studies Since 1942." *The Book Encompassed: Studies in Twentieth-Century Bibliography*, edited by Peter Davison, Oak Knoll Press, 1998, pp. 24–36.

Tennis, Joseph T. "Is There a New Bibliography?" *Cataloging & Classification Quarterly*, vol. 49, no. 2, 2011, pp. 121–26, https://doi.org/10.1080/01639374.2011.544020.

Teufel, Simone, and Marc Moens. "Summarizing Scientific Articles: Experiments with Relevance and Rhetorical Status." *Computational Linguistics*, vol. 28, no. 4, 2002, pp. 409–45, https://doi.org/10.1162/089120102762671936.

The University of Chicago Press Editorial Sta, editor. *The Chicago Manual of Style*. 17th ed., University of Chicago Press, 2017, https://doi.org/10.7208/cmos17.

Van Hoesen, Henry Bartlett. *Bibliography: Practical, Enumerative, Historical: An Introductory Manual*. Burt Franklin, 1971.

Wang, Zheng (John). "Co-Curation: New Strategies, Roles, Services, and Opportunities for Libraries in the Post-Web Era and the Digital Media Context." *Libri*, vol. 63, no. 2, 2013, pp. 71–86, https://doi.org/10.1515/libri-2013-0006.

White, Howard D. "Literary Forms in Information Work: Annotated Bibliographies, Bibliographic Essays, and Reviews of Literatures." *For Information Specialists: Interpretations of Reference and Bibliographic Work*, edited by Howard D. White et al., Ablex Publishing Corporation, 1994, pp. 131–49.

Wigmore, Ethel. "On Making and Using a Bibliography." *The American Journal of Nursing*, vol. 36, no. 5, 1936, pp. 463–68, https://doi.org/10.2307/3412201.

Zarobila, Charles. "Definition and Description of Bibliography." *Bibliography in Literature, Folklore, Language, and Linguistics: Essays on the Status of the Field*, edited by David William Foster and James R. Kelly, McFarland & Company, Inc., 2003, pp. 5–18.

Zerby, Chuck. *The Devil's Details: A History of Footnotes*. Simon & Schuster, 2003.

2 The Annotated Bibliography in Higher Education

Luke Beatty

Introduction

This chapter is a thematically organized bibliography on the uses of annotated bibliographies (ABs) in higher education. To gather material, I performed an English-language search for academic and professional literature about [annotated bibliographies] AND [pedagogy/classrooms/libraries] AND [higher education/ colleges/universities/other variants]. I searched across the following platforms...

- A variety of EBSCO, Gale, and ProQuest databases
- The Consortium of Academic and Research Libraries in Illinois' unified library catalogue
- *Google Scholar* and *Google*

... and identified 116 items containing non-trivial discussions of ABs in higher education. Of these, 79 were academic or professional journal articles; 32 were books or book chapters; and 5 were miscellaneous scholarly items. Web-published "how-to" guides, sample ABs, *LibGuides*, and other library help materials were excluded from the search. Though select sources were weeded for reasons of quality and fit, most of the items I identified appear in the bibliography below. To organize the bibliography, I faceted the literature into eight analytical categories – with some overlap between categories – and briefly annotated each category to give readers a sense of my faceting logic. To the best of my knowledge, this is the most comprehensive bibliography about ABs in higher education.

DOI: 10.4324/9781003214434-2

Manuals and Skill Books

This category contains AB literature for students and instructors. The sources typically explain the form, purpose, and practicalities of AB writing.

This first grouping contains comprehensive book-length works (and one article) that fulsomely explain the AB.

Avery, Heather, and Paul Gamache. *Proposals & Annotated Bibliographies: An Essential Skills Guide*. 2nd ed., Trent University, 2003.

Beatty, Luke, and Cynthia A. Cochran. *Writing the Annotated Bibliography: A Guide for Students and Researchers*. Routledge, 2020, https://doi.org/10.4324/9780367853051.

Eula, Michael J., and Janet Madden. *Compiling the Annotated Bibliography: A Guide*. 2nd ed., Kendall/Hunt Publishing Company, 1995.

Gentile, Angela. "Annotated Bibliographies for Dummies." *Grassroots Writing Research Journal*, vol. 2, no. 2, 2012, pp. 65–71, https://is.gd/L0dYlc.

Harner, James L. *On Compiling an Annotated Bibliography*. 2nd ed., Modern Language Association of America, 2000.

Non-Formal Education Information Center. *Preparing Citations and Annotations*. Michigan State University, 1983.

This next grouping contains representative examples of student-facing books with sections about ABs.

These sections are typically short – often no more than a few pages – but they give students a brief overview of how to write ABs.

Baker, Cassandra. *Key Tools of Writing & Research: A Guide for the Student Writer*. Kendall Hunt Publishing Company, 2020.

Ballenger, Bruce P. *The Curious Writer*. 5th ed., Pearson, 2017.

Bergmann, Linda S. *Academic Research and Writing: Inquiry and Argument in College*. Longman, 2010.

Hacker, Diana, and Nancy I. Sommers. *The Bedford Handbook*. 11 ed., Bedford/St. Martin's, 2020.

Pike, David L. *What Every Student Should Know About... Writing About World Literature*. Pearson Education, 2011.

This final grouping lists works for academic librarians, bibliographers, and other academic professionals.

They inform the reader about how to write, compile, and annotate ABs.

Berger, Sidney E. "Annotations." *The Design of Bibliographies: Observations, References, and Examples*, Greenwood Press, 1992, pp. 35–36.

Colaianne, Anthony Joseph. "The Aims and Methods of Annotated Bibliography." *Scholarly Publishing*, vol. 11, no. 4, 1980, pp. 321–31.
Krummel, Donald William. "Annotation." *Bibliographies: Their Aims and Methods*, H.W. Wilson Co., 1984, pp. 75–84.
Long, Liza, et al. "Tracking Research with Annotated Bibliographies." *Write What Matters*. MSL Academic Endeavors, 2020, pp. 1047–60, https://is.gd/qbNeBX.
Menapace, John. "Some Approaches to Annotation." *Scholarly Publishing*, vol. 1, no. 2, 1970, pp. 194–205.
Wheeler, Helen Rippier. *The Bibliographic Instruction-Course Handbook: A Skills and Concepts Approach to the Undergraduate, Research Methodology, Credit Course - For College and University Personnel*. Scarecrow Press, 1988.

Librarian and Instructor Collaboration

This category contains works about librarians who assign ABs either in collaboration with instructors or individually in their courses. This first grouping includes works about librarian-instructor collaborations.

Birkett, Melissa, and Amy Hughes. "A Collaborative Project to Integrate Information Literacy Skills into an Undergraduate Psychology Course." *Psychology Learning & Teaching*, vol. 12, no. 1, 2013, pp. 96–100, https://doi.org/10.2304/plat.2013.12.1.96.
Brinkman, Stacy N., and Arianne A. Hartsell-Gundy. "Building Trust to Relieve Graduate Student Research Anxiety." *Public Services Quarterly*, vol. 8, no. 1, 2012, pp. 26–39, https://doi.org/10.1080/15228959.2011.591680.
Callas, Jennie E. "Assessing One-Shot Instruction: Using Post-Assignment Evaluations to Build Better Assignments." *Thirty-Sixth National LOEX Library Instruction Conference Proceedings: Librarian as Architect: Planning, Building, & Renewing*, edited by Brad Sietz, LOEX Press, 2010, pp. 35–39, https://is.gd/0BK2LE.
Diamond, Kelly. "Problem-Based Learning and Information Literacy: Revising a Technical Writing Class." *Teaching Information Literacy and Writing Studies: Volume 2, Upper-Level and Graduate Courses*, edited by Grace Veach, Purdue University Press, 2019, pp. 157–68, https://doi.org/10.2307/j.ctv15wxqwx.15.
Dinkelman, Andrea L., et al. "Using an Interdisciplinary Approach to Teach Undergraduates Communication and Information Literacy Skills." *Journal of Natural Resources and Life Sciences Education*, vol. 39, no. 1, 2010, pp. 137–44, https://doi.org/doi:10.4195/jnrlse.2010.0005u.
Duerr, Larry, and Jodi Eastberg. "Beyond the Annotated Bibliography: Engaging Students with Library Collections." *College & Research Libraries News*, vol. 73, no. 8, 2012, pp. 478–80, https://doi.org/10.5860/crln.73.8.8815.

Dunne, Siobhan, and Vera Sheridan. "Developing First Year Student Information Literacy: Reflections on the Learning Process." *All Ireland Journal of Teaching and Learning in Higher Education*, vol. 4, no. 1, 2012, https://is.gd/TtELYa.

Edwards, Mary E., and Erik W. Black. "Contemporary Instructor-Librarian Collaboration: A Case Study of an Online Embedded Librarian Implementation." *Journal of Library & Information Services in Distance Learning*, vol. 6, no. 3–4, 2012, pp. 284–311, https://doi.org/10.1080/1533290X.2012.705690.

Edwards, Mary, et al. "Assessing the Value of Embedded Librarians in an Online Graduate Educational Technology Course." *Public Services Quarterly*, vol. 6, no. 2–3, 2010, pp. 271–91, http://dx.doi.org/10.1080/15228959.2010.497447.

Flaspohler, Molly R., et al. "The Annotated Bibliography and Citation Behavior: Enhancing Student Scholarship in an Undergraduate Biology Course." *CBE—Life Sciences Education*, vol. 6, no. 4, 2007, pp. 350–60, https://doi.org/10.1187/cbe.07-04-0022.

Laskin, Miriam, and Cynthia R. Haller. "Up the Mountain without a Trail: Helping Students Use Source Networks to Find Their Way." *Information Literacy: Research and Collaboration Across Disciplines*, edited by Barbara J. D'Angelo et al., The WAC Clearinghouse / University Press of Colorado, 2017, pp. 237–56, https://doi.org/10.37514/PER-B.2016.0834.2.11.

Miller, Ielleen R. "Turning the Tables: A Faculty-Centered Approach to Integrating Information Literacy." *Reference Services Review*, vol. 38, no. 4, 2010, pp. 647–62, https://doi.org/10.1108/00907321011090782.

Mussleman, Paul, and Ellen B. Buckner. "Information Literacy as a Co-Requisite to Critical Thinking: A Librarian and Educator Partnership." *The Other Culture: Science and Mathematics Education in Honors*, edited by Ellen B. Buckner and Keith Garbutt, National Collegiate Honors Council, 2012, pp. 39–52, https://is.gd/jXmJgH.

Paglia, Alison, and Annie Donahue. "Collaboration Works: Integrating Information Competencies into the Psychology Curricula." *Reference Services Review*, vol. 31, no. 4, 2003, pp. 320–28, https://doi.org/10.1108/00907320310505618.

Rinto, Erin E. "Developing and Applying an Information Literacy Rubric to Student Annotated Bibliographies." *Evidence Based Library and Information Practice*, vol. 8, no. 3, 2013, pp. 5–18, https://doi.org/10.18438/B8559F.

Rinto, Erin E., and Elisa I. Cogbill-Seiders. "Library Instruction and Themed Composition Courses: An Investigation of Factors That Impact Student Learning." *The Journal of Academic Librarianship*, vol. 41, no. 1, 2015, pp. 14–20, https://doi.org/10.1016/j.acalib.2014.11.010.

Roberson, Julie, and Jenny Horton. "Creating a Combination IL and English Composition Course in a College Setting." *Best Practices for*

The Annotated Bibliography in Higher Education 13

Credit-Bearing Information Literacy Courses, edited by Christopher Vance Hollister, Association of College and Research Libraries, 2010, pp. 65–76, https://is.gd/wrHM6F.

Simons, Alexandra C. "Librarians, Faculty, and the Writing Center Partnering to Build an Interdisciplinary Course: A Case Study at the University of Houston, USA." *New Review of Academic Librarianship*, vol. 23, no. 1, 2017, pp. 28–41, https://doi.org/10.1080/13614533.2016.1185020.

Walsh, Lynda, et al. "The Burkean Parlor as Boundary Object: A Collaboration between First-Year Writing and the Library." *Composition Studies*, vol. 46, no. 1, 2018, pp. 103–23, https://is.gd/NEXHZH.

Williams, Michelle Hale, et al. "Weighing the Research Paper Option: The Difference That Information Literacy Skills Can Make." *PS: Political Science and Politics*, vol. 39, no. 3, 2006, pp. 513–19, https://is.gd/gQFJk8.

This second grouping includes works about AB assignments in courses taught solely by academic librarians.

Armstrong, Jeanne, and Margaret Fast. "A Credit Course Assignment: The Encyclopedia Entry." *Reference Services Review*, vol. 32, no. 2, 2004, pp. 190–94, https://doi.org/10.1108/00907320410537711.

Daugman, Ellen, et al. "Designing and Implementing an Information Literacy Course in the Humanities." *Communications in Information Literacy*, vol. 5, no. 2, 2012, pp. 127–43, https://doi.org/10.15760/comminfolit.2012.5.2.108.

Faix, Allison. "Assisting Students to Identify Sources: An Investigation." *Library Review*, vol. 63, no. 8/9, 2014, pp. 624–36, https://doi.org/10.1108/LR-07-2013-0100.

Finch, Jannette L., and Renée N. Jefferson. "Designing Authentic Learning Tasks for Online Library Instruction." *The Journal of Academic Librarianship*, vol. 39, no. 2, 2013, pp. 181–88, https://doi.org/10.1016/j.acalib.2012.10.005.

Gauder, Heidi, and Fred Jenkins. "Engaging Undergraduates in Discipline-Based Research." *Reference Services Review*, vol. 40, no. 2, 2012, pp. 277–94, https://doi.org/10.1108/00907321211228327.

Hosier, Allison. "Teaching Information Literacy through 'Un-Research.'" *Communications in Information Literacy*, vol. 9, no. 2, 2015, pp. 126–35, https://doi.org/10.15760/comminfolit.2015.9.2.189.

Johnson, Catherine, et al. "Integrating the Credit Information Literacy Course into a Learning Community." *Best Practices for Credit-Bearing Information Literacy Courses*, edited by Christopher Vance Hollister, Association of College and Research Libraries, 2010, pp. 53–63, https://is.gd/wrHM6F.

Lantz, Catherine, et al. "Student Bibliographies: Charting Research Skills over Time." *Reference Services Review*, vol. 44, no. 3, 2016, pp. 253–65, https://doi.org/10.1108/RSR-12-2015-0053.

Mounce, Michael. "Teaching Information Literacy at Delta State University." *The Southeastern Librarian*, vol. 54, no. 3, 2006, pp. 35–41, https://is.gd/CXJ9Rv.

Mounce, Michael. "Teaching Information Literacy Online: One Librarian's Experience." *Delta Journal of Education*, vol. 3, no. 2, 2013, pp. 102–13, https://is.gd/5ZC0wi.

Newell, William H., et al. "Distinctive Challenges of Library-Based Interdisciplinary Research and Writing: A Guide." *Issues in Integrative Studies*, no. 25, 2007, pp. 84–110, https://is.gd/36qj1N.

Patterson, David Jay. *Becoming Researchers: Community College ESL Students, Information Literacy, and the Library*. UC Berkeley, 2011, https://is.gd/py6wK7.

First-Year Writing and General Education Courses

Because many undergraduates have difficulty with longform writing, ABs are often assigned in first-year writing and general education classes in lieu of, or in addition to, research papers. This category contains works discussing AB assignments used in first-year writing and general education courses.

Aull, Laura. "Corpus Analysis of Argumentative Versus Explanatory Discourse in Writing Task Genres." *The Journal of Writing Analytics*, vol. 1, no. 1, 2017, pp. 1–47, https://doi.org/10.37514/JWA-J.2017.1.1.03.

Bodi, Sonia. "Relevance in Library Instruction: The Pursuit." *College & Research Libraries*, vol. 45, no. 1, 1984, pp. 59–65, https://doi.org/10.5860/crl_45_01_59.

Callas, Jennie E. "Assessing One-Shot Instruction: Using Post-Assignment Evaluations to Build Better Assignments." *Thirty-Sixth National LOEX Library Instruction Conference Proceedings: Librarian as Architect: Planning, Building, & Renewing*, edited by Brad Sietz, LOEX Press, 2010, pp. 35–39, https://is.gd/0BK2LE.

Carbery, Alan, and Sean Leahy. "Evidence-Based Instruction: Assessing Student Work Using Rubrics and Citation Analysis to Inform Instructional Design." *Journal of Information Literacy*, vol. 9, no. 1, 2015, pp. 74–90, https://doi.org/10.11645/9.1.1980.

Dunne, Siobhan, and Vera Sheridan. "Developing First Year Student Information Literacy: Reflections on the Learning Process." *All Ireland Journal of Teaching and Learning in Higher Education*, vol. 4, no. 1, 2012, https://is.gd/TtELYa.

Insua, Glenda M., et al. "In Their Own Words: Using First-Year Student Research Journals to Guide Information Literacy Instruction." *Portal: Libraries and the Academy*, vol. 18, no. 1, 2018, pp. 141–61, https://doi.org/10.1353/pla.2018.0007.

Jones, Leigh A. "Podcasting and Performativity: Multimodal Invention in an Advanced Writing Class." *Composition Studies*, vol. 38, no. 2, 2010, pp. 75-91, https://is.gd/bHN2aA.

Montgomery, Susan. "Alternatives to the Annotated Bibliography." *ROLLINSpire: News & Inspiration from the Endeavor Foundation Center for Faculty Development*, 26 Feb. 2021, https://is.gd/lL0HGN.

Richter, Jacob D. "Assessing, Deliberating, Responding: An Annotated Bibliography for a Post-Truth Age." *Prompt: A Journal of Academic Writing Assignments*, vol. 4, no. 2, 2020, pp. 23-36, https://doi.org/10.31719/pjaw.v4i2.79.

Risanti, Yanidya Ulfa. "The Undergraduate Students Critical Thinking in Writing Evaluative Annotated Bibliography in Extensive Reading Class." *RETAIN: Research on English Language Teaching in Indonesia*, vol. 7, no. 1, 2019, pp. 80-89, https://is.gd/hRkUon.

Russom, Caroline L. "First Year Research and Writing Convergences." *Academic Exchange Quarterly*, vol. 7, no. 3, 2003, pp. 194-98.

Tan-de Ramos, Jennifer. "Effects of Teaching Strategies in Annotated Bibliography Writing." *Journal of Education and Practice*, vol. 6, no. 7, 2015, pp. 54-57, https://is.gd/uFU4KD.

Walsh, Lynda, et al. "The Burkean Parlor as Boundary Object: A Collaboration between First-Year Writing and the Library." *Composition Studies*, vol. 46, no. 1, 2018, pp. 103-23, https://is.gd/NEXHZH.

Humanities and Social Sciences

This category lists works about AB assignments in the humanities and social sciences.

Bassett, Penny. "How Do Students View Asynchronous Online Discussions as a Learning Experience?" *Interdisciplinary Journal of E-Skills and Lifelong Learning*, vol. 7, 2011, pp. 69-79, https://doi.org/10.28945/1376.

Berry, Bridget, et al. "'It's a Practice Thing': The Annotated Bibliography as a Learning Activity for Arts Students." *Synergy*, no. 31, 2011, pp. 24-31, https://is.gd/nx8Hku.

Bobkowski, Piotr S., and Karna Younger. "News Credibility: Adapting and Testing a Source Evaluation Assessment in Journalism." *College & Research Libraries*, vol. 81, no. 5, 2020, pp. 822-43, https://doi.org/10.5860/crl.81.5.822.

Brinkman, Stacy N., and Arianne A. Hartsell-Gundy. "Building Trust to Relieve Graduate Student Research Anxiety." *Public Services Quarterly*, vol. 8, no. 1, 2012, pp. 26-39, https://doi.org/10.1080/15228959.2011.591680.

Cameron, Jeanne, et al. "Assessment as Critical Praxis: A Community College Experience." *Teaching Sociology*, vol. 30, 2002, pp. 414-29, https://doi.org/10.2307/3211502.

Charles, Leslin H., and William DeFabiis. "Closing the Transactional Distance in an Online Graduate Course through the Practice of Embedded Librarianship." *College & Research Libraries*, vol. 82, no. 3, 2021, pp. 370–88, https://doi.org/10.5860/crl.82.3.370.

Duerr, Larry, and Jodi Eastberg. "Beyond the Annotated Bibliography: Engaging Students with Library Collections." *College & Research Libraries News*, vol. 73, no. 8, 2012, pp. 478–80, https://doi.org/10.5860/crln.73.8.8815.

Jensen, Erin B. "Writing in the Social Sciences." *Syllabus*, vol. 6, no. 1, 2017, pp. 1–10, https://is.gd/A1Z3Or.

King-O'Brien, Kelly, et al. "Reimagining Writing in History Courses." *Journal of American History*, vol. 107, no. 4, 2021, pp. 942–54, https://doi.org/10.1093/jahist/jaaa465.

Leigh, Jennifer S. A., and Cynthia A. Gibbon. "Information Literacy and the Introductory Management Classroom." *Journal of Management Education*, vol. 32, no. 4, 2008, pp. 509–30, https://doi.org/10.1177/1052562908317023.

Lidzy, Sheryl. "'Doing Business In...': An Emic Training Module." *Journal of the Communication, Speech & Theatre Association of North Dakota*, vol. 23, 2011/2010, pp. 49–55.

Mostert, Linda Ann, and Rodwell Townsend. "Embedding the Teaching of Academic Writing into Anthropology Lectures." *Innovations in Education and Teaching International*, vol. 55, no. 1, 2018, pp. 82–90, https://doi.org/10.1080/14703297.2016.1231619.

Muñoz, Caroline Lego. "More than Just Wikipedia: Creating a Collaborative Research Library Using a Wiki." *Marketing Education Review*, vol. 22, no. 1, 2012, pp. 21–26, https://doi.org/10.2753/MER1052-8008220104.

Parkes, Mitchell, et al. "Collaborative Annotated Bibliographies: An Online Strategy to Foster Student Collaboration and Understanding." *Proceedings of EdMedia 2013--World Conference on Educational Media and Technology*, Association for the Advancement of Computing in Education (AACE), 2013, pp. 2205–11, https://is.gd/x7QUzh.

Pashaie, Billy. "Teaching Research for Academic Purposes." *The CATESOL Journal*, vol. 21, no. 1, 2010/2009, pp. 162–74, https://is.gd/o2w1Hv.

Patterson, David Jay. *Becoming Researchers: Community College ESL Students, Information Literacy, and the Library*. UC Berkeley, 2011, https://is.gd/py6wK7.

Williams, Michelle Hale, et al. "Weighing the Research Paper Option: The Difference That Information Literacy Skills Can Make." *PS: Political Science and Politics*, vol. 39, no. 3, 2006, pp. 513–19, https://is.gd/gQFJk8.

Winicki, Barbara Ann. "Reading Teachers and Research: From Consumers to Evaluators to Producers." *Journal of Reading Education*, vol. 31, no. 2, 2006, pp. 21–28.

Winslow, Rachel Rains, et al. "Not Just for Citations: Assessing Zotero While Reassessing Research." *Information Literacy: Research and*

Collaboration Across Disciplines, edited by Barbara J. D'Angelo et al., The WAC Clearinghouse / University Press of Colorado, 2017, pp. 287–304, https://doi.org/10.37514/PER-B.2016.0834.2.14.

Hard Sciences

This category includes works about AB assignments used in mathematics, hard sciences, and allied health fields.

Birkett, Melissa, and Amy Hughes. "A Collaborative Project to Integrate Information Literacy Skills into an Undergraduate Psychology Course." *Psychology Learning & Teaching*, vol. 12, no. 1, 2013, pp. 96–100, https://doi.org/10.2304/plat.2013.12.1.96.

Coulson, Michelle. "Annotated Bibliographies Can Help Maximise Benefit of Literature Research Skills Exercises." *Proceedings of The Australian Conference on Science and Mathematics Education*, edited by Australian Conference on Science and Mathematics Education, Australian Conference on Science and Mathematics Education, 2007, pp. 160–63, https://is.gd/Cz6Ofw.

Croft, James, et al. "Writing in the Disciplines and Student Pre-Professional Identity: An Exploratory Study." *Across the Disciplines*, vol. 16, no. 2, 2019, pp. 1–20, https://doi.org/10.37514/ATD-J.2019.16.2.09.

Digh, Andy D. "Writing and Speech Instruction in an Introductory Artificial Intelligence Course." *Journal of Computing Sciences in Colleges*, vol. 36, no. 5, 2021, pp. 119–28, https://doi.org/10.5555/3447307.3447318.

Everly, James, and Laura Wilson. "Weaving The Capstone Tapestry." *2007 Annual Conference & Exposition Proceedings*, American Society for Engineering Education, 2007, pp. 12.1597.1–12.1597.20, https://doi.org/10.18260/1-2--2270.

Flaspohler, Molly R., et al. "The Annotated Bibliography and Citation Behavior: Enhancing Student Scholarship in an Undergraduate Biology Course." *CBE—Life Sciences Education*, vol. 6, no. 4, 2007, pp. 350–60, https://doi.org/10.1187/cbe.07-04-0022.

Franzen, Susan, and Colleen Bannon. "Merging Information Literacy and Evidence-Based Practice in an Undergraduate Health Sciences Curriculum Map." *Communications in Information Literacy*, vol. 10, no. 2, 2016, pp. 245–63, https://doi.org/10.15760/comminfolit.2016.10.2.26.

Gigante, Maria E. "Critical Science Literacy for Science Majors: Introducing Future Scientists to the Communicative Arts." *Bulletin of Science, Technology & Society*, vol. 34, no. 3–4, 2014, pp. 77–86, https://doi.org/10.1177/0270467614556090.

Goodman, Xan, et al. "Applying an Information Literacy Rubric to First-Year Health Sciences Student Research Posters." *Journal of the*

Medical Library Association, vol. 106, no. 1, 2018, pp. 108–12, https://doi.org/10.5195/JMLA.2018.400.

Knox, Kerry J., et al. "A Positive Student Experience of Collaborative Project Work in Upper-Year Undergraduate Chemistry." *Chemistry Education Research and Practice*, vol. 20, no. 2, 2019, pp. 340–57, https://doi.org/10.1039/C8RP00251G.

McDaniel, Jodi, and Joni Tornwall. "Authentic Engagement in High-Enrollment Graduate Courses: Pathophysiology Consumers Become Content Creators." *Nurse Educator*, vol. 41, no. 3, 2016, pp. 151–55, https://doi.org/10.1097/NNE.0000000000000223.

Mussleman, Paul, and Ellen B. Buckner. "Information Literacy as a Co-Requisite to Critical Thinking: A Librarian and Educator Partnership." *The Other Culture: Science and Mathematics Education in Honors*, edited by Ellen B. Buckner and Keith Garbutt, National Collegiate Honors Council, 2012, pp. 39–52, https://is.gd/jXmJgH.

Paglia, Alison, and Annie Donahue. "Collaboration Works: Integrating Information Competencies into the Psychology Curricula." *Reference Services Review*, vol. 31, no. 4, 2003, pp. 320–28, https://doi.org/10.1108/00907320310505618.

Rose-Wiles, Lisa, et al. "Enhancing Information Literacy Using Bernard Lonergan's Generalized Empirical Method: A Three-Year Case Study in a First Year Biology Course." *The Journal of Academic Librarianship*, vol. 43, 2017, pp. 495–508, http://dx.doi.org/10.1016/j.acalib.2017.08.012.

Tsunekage, Toshi, et al. "Integrating Information Literacy Training into an Inquiry-Based Introductory Biology Laboratory." *Journal of Biological Education*, vol. 54, no. 4, 2020, pp. 396–403, https://doi.org/10.1080/00219266.2019.1600569.

Whatley, Kara. "Making Instruction Audience-Appropriate: Information Literacy for Non-Traditional Students." *Brick and Click Libraries: An Academic Library Symposium*, edited by Frank Baudino et al., Northwest Missouri State University, 2006, pp. 100–04.

Wolfe, Kate S. "Emerging Information Literacy and Research-Method Competencies in Urban Community College Psychology Students." *Community College Enterprise*, vol. 21, no. 2, 2015, pp. 93–99, https://is.gd/MoqDnX.

Scaffolding

This category includes works wherein ABs are discussed as scaffolding tools leading to subsequent assignments.

The most common AB follow-up assignment is the research paper, though others are also discussed.

Cameron, Jeanne, et al. "Assessment as Critical Praxis: A Community College Experience." *Teaching Sociology*, vol. 30, 2002, pp. 414–29, https://doi.org/10.2307/3211502.

Digh, Andy D. "Writing and Speech Instruction in an Introductory Artificial Intelligence Course." *Journal of Computing Sciences in Colleges*, vol. 36, no. 5, 2021, pp. 119–28, https://doi.org/10.5555/3447307.3447318.
Insua, Glenda M., et al. "In Their Own Words: Using First-Year Student Research Journals to Guide Information Literacy Instruction." *Portal: Libraries and the Academy*, vol. 18, no. 1, 2018, pp. 141–61, https://doi.org/10.1353/pla.2018.0007.
Jensen, Erin B. "Writing in the Social Sciences." *Syllabus*, vol. 6, no. 1, 2017, pp. 1–10, https://is.gd/A1Z3Or.
Jones, Leigh A. "Podcasting and Performativity: Multimodal Invention in an Advanced Writing Class." *Composition Studies*, vol. 38, no. 2, 2010, pp. 75–91, https://is.gd/bHN2aA.
Koss, Lorelei. "Writing and Information Literacy in a Cryptology First-Year Seminar." *Cryptologia*, vol. 38, no. 3, 2014, pp. 223–31, https://doi.org/10.1080/01611194.2014.915256.
Laskin, Miriam, and Cynthia R. Haller. "Up the Mountain without a Trail: Helping Students Use Source Networks to Find Their Way." *Information Literacy: Research and Collaboration Across Disciplines*, edited by Barbara J. D'Angelo et al., The WAC Clearinghouse / University Press of Colorado, 2017, pp. 237–56, https://doi.org/10.37514/PER-B.2016.0834.2.11.
Lidzy, Sheryl. "'Doing Business In...': An Emic Training Module." *Journal of the Communication, Speech & Theatre Association of North Dakota*, vol. 23, 2011/2010, pp. 49–55.
Rose-Wiles, Lisa, et al. "Enhancing Information Literacy Using Bernard Lonergan's Generalized Empirical Method: A Three-Year Case Study in a First Year Biology Course." *The Journal of Academic Librarianship*, vol. 43, 2017, pp. 495–508, http://dx.doi.org/10.1016/j.acalib.2017.08.012.
Russom, Caroline L. "First Year Research and Writing Convergences." *Academic Exchange Quarterly*, vol. 7, no. 3, 2003, pp. 194–98.
Vaughan, Michelle, et al. "Connecting the Dots: A Scaffolded Model for Undergraduate Research." *National FORUM of Teacher Education Journal*, vol. 27, no. 3, 2017, https://is.gd/HtVKF6.

Student Learning and Assessment

This category includes works that conceptualize ABs as tools to develop information literacy or assess student learning.

The first grouping includes works that explain how effective AB assignments were at developing information literacy skills.

Berry, Bridget, et al. "'It's a Practice Thing': The Annotated Bibliography as a Learning Activity for Arts Students." *Synergy*, no. 31, 2011, pp. 24–31, https://is.gd/nx8Hku.
Blackwell-Starnes, Katt. "Preliminary Paths to Information Literacy: Introducing Research in Core Courses." *Information Literacy: Research*

and Collaboration Across Disciplines, edited by Barbara J. D'Angelo et al., The WAC Clearinghouse / University Press of Colorado, 2017, pp. 139–61, https://doi.org/10.37514/PER-B.2016.0834.2.07.

Engeldinger, Eugene A. "Bibliographic Instruction and Critical Thinking: The Contribution of the Annotated Bibliography." *Reference Quarterly (RQ)*, vol. 28, no. 2, 1988, pp. 95–102, https://is.gd/aaCGfa.

Faix, Allison. "Assisting Students to Identify Sources: An Investigation." *Library Review*, vol. 63, no. 8/9, 2014, pp. 624–36, https://doi.org/10.1108/LR-07-2013-0100.

Flaspohler, Molly R., et al. "The Annotated Bibliography and Citation Behavior: Enhancing Student Scholarship in an Undergraduate Biology Course." *CBE—Life Sciences Education*, vol. 6, no. 4, 2007, pp. 350–60, https://doi.org/10.1187/cbe.07-04-0022.

Goodman, Xan, et al. "Applying an Information Literacy Rubric to First-Year Health Sciences Student Research Posters." *Journal of the Medical Library Association*, vol. 106, no. 1, 2018, pp. 108–12, https://doi.org/10.5195/JMLA.2018.400.

Hemminger, Bradley M., and Julia TerMaat. "Annotating for the World: Attitudes toward Sharing Scholarly Annotations." *Journal of the Association for Information Science and Technology*, vol. 65, no. 11, 2014, pp. 2278–92, https://doi.org/10.1002/asi.23124.

Johnson, Catherine, et al. "Integrating the Credit Information Literacy Course into a Learning Community." *Best Practices for Credit-Bearing Information Literacy Courses*, edited by Christopher Vance Hollister, Association of College and Research Libraries, 2010, pp. 53–63, https://is.gd/wrHM6F.

Lantz, Catherine, et al. "Student Bibliographies: Charting Research Skills Over Time." *Reference Services Review*, vol. 44, no. 3, 2016, pp. 253–65, https://doi.org/10.1108/RSR-12-2015-0053.

Mills, Jenny, et al. "Beyond the Checklist Approach: A Librarian-Faculty Collaboration to Teach the BEAM Method of Source Evaluation." *Communications in Information Literacy*, vol. 15, no. 1, 2021, pp. 119–39, https://doi.org/10.15760/comminfolit.2021.15.1.7.

Mostert, Linda Ann, and Rodwell Townsend. "Embedding the Teaching of Academic Writing into Anthropology Lectures." *Innovations in Education and Teaching International*, vol. 55, no. 1, 2018, pp. 82–90, https://doi.org/10.1080/14703297.2016.1231619.

Tan-de Ramos, Jennifer. "Effects of Teaching Strategies in Annotated Bibliography Writing." *Journal of Education and Practice*, vol. 6, no. 7, 2015, pp. 54–57, https://is.gd/uFU4KD.

This second grouping includes works analyzing the effectiveness of ABs as learning assessment tools.

Aull, Laura. "Corpus Analysis of Argumentative Versus Explanatory Discourse in Writing Task Genres." *The Journal of Writing Analytics*, vol. 1, no. 1, 2017, pp. 1–47, https://doi.org/10.37514/JWA-J.2017.1.1.03.

Cameron, Jeanne, et al. "Assessment as Critical Praxis: A Community College Experience." *Teaching Sociology*, vol. 30, 2002, pp. 414–29, https://doi.org/10.2307/3211502.

Carbery, Alan, and Sean Leahy. "Evidence-Based Instruction: Assessing Student Work Using Rubrics and Citation Analysis to Inform Instructional Design." *Journal of Information Literacy*, vol. 9, no. 1, 2015, pp. 74–90, https://doi.org/10.11645/9.1.1980.

McGowan, Britt, et al. "What Do Undergraduate Course Syllabi Say about Information Literacy?" *Portal: Libraries and the Academy*, vol. 16, no. 3, 2016, pp. 599–617, https://doi.org/10.1353/pla.2016.0040.

Parkes, Mitchell, et al. "Collaborative Annotated Bibliographies: An Online Strategy to Foster Student Collaboration and Understanding." *Proceedings of EdMedia 2013--World Conference on Educational Media and Technology*, Association for the Advancement of Computing in Education (AACE), 2013, pp. 2205–11, https://is.gd/x7QUzh.

Rinto, Erin E. "Developing and Applying an Information Literacy Rubric to Student Annotated Bibliographies." *Evidence Based Library and Information Practice*, vol. 8, no. 3, 2013, pp. 5–18, https://doi.org/10.18438/B8559F.

Rinto, Erin E., and Elisa I. Cogbill-Seiders. "Library Instruction and Themed Composition Courses: An Investigation of Factors That Impact Student Learning." *The Journal of Academic Librarianship*, vol. 41, no. 1, 2015, pp. 14–20, https://doi.org/10.1016/j.acalib.2014.11.010.

Online and Web

This category includes works that discuss the use of AB assignments and social annotation in online learning.

This first grouping lists works about the use of ABs in remote learning and the online production of ABs using technologies such as *Zotero* or *Hypothesis*.

Bassett, Penny. "How Do Students View Asynchronous Online Discussions as a Learning Experience?" *Interdisciplinary Journal of E-Skills and Lifelong Learning*, vol. 7, 2011, pp. 69–79, https://doi.org/10.28945/1376.

Charles, Leslin H., and William DeFabiis. "Closing the Transactional Distance in an Online Graduate Course through the Practice of Embedded Librarianship." *College & Research Libraries*, vol. 82, no. 3, 2021, pp. 370–88, https://doi.org/10.5860/crl.82.3.370.

Edwards, Mary E., and Erik W. Black. "Contemporary Instructor-Librarian Collaboration: A Case Study of an Online Embedded Librarian Implementation." *Journal of Library & Information Services in Distance Learning*, vol. 6, no. 3–4, 2012, pp. 284–311, https://doi.org/10.1080/1533290X.2012.705690.

Edwards, Mary, et al. "Assessing the Value of Embedded Librarians in an Online Graduate Educational Technology Course." *Public Services Quarterly*, vol. 6, no. 2–3, 2010, pp. 271–91, http://dx.doi.org/10.1080/15228959.2010.497447.

Finch, Jannette L., and Renée N. Jefferson. "Designing Authentic Learning Tasks for Online Library Instruction." *The Journal of Academic Librarianship*, vol. 39, no. 2, 2013, pp. 181–88, https://doi.org/10.1016/j.acalib.2012.10.005.

Hemminger, Bradley M., and Julia TerMaat. "Annotating for the World: Attitudes toward Sharing Scholarly Annotations." *Journal of the Association for Information Science and Technology*, vol. 65, no. 11, 2014, pp. 2278–92, https://doi.org/10.1002/asi.23124.

Jumonville, Anne. "The Humanities in Process, Not Crisis: Information Literacy as a Means of Low-Stakes Course Innovation." *College & Research Libraries News*, vol. 75, no. 2, 2014, pp. 84–87, https://doi.org/10.5860/crln.75.2.9072.

King-O'Brien, Kelly, et al. "Reimagining Writing in History Courses." *Journal of American History*, vol. 107, no. 4, 2021, pp. 942–54, https://doi.org/10.1093/jahist/jaaa465.

Kumar, Swapna, et al. "Analysis of Online Students' Use of Embedded Library Instruction in a Graduate Educational Technology Course." *Proceedings of E-Learn: World Conference on E-Learning in Corporate, Government, Healthcare, and Higher Education*, Association for the Advancement of Computing in Education, 2010, pp. 664–71, https://is.gd/jYZiAm.

Parkes, Mitchell, et al. "Collaborative Annotated Bibliographies: An Online Strategy to Foster Student Collaboration and Understanding." *Proceedings of EdMedia 2013--World Conference on Educational Media and Technology*, Association for the Advancement of Computing in Education (AACE), 2013, pp. 2205–11, https://is.gd/x7QUzh.

Sample, Mark. "Sharing Research and Building Knowledge through Zotero." *Learning Through Digital Media: Experiments in Technology and Pedagogy*, edited by R. Trebor Scholz, Institute for Distributed Creativity, 2011, pp. 295–303, https://is.gd/Hf43eE.

Stadler, Derek. *Writing Effective Annotated Bibliographies Using Blackboard's Discussion Board*. CUNY La Guardia Community College, 2018, https://is.gd/Ylry7P.

Winslow, Rachel Rains, et al. "Not Just for Citations: Assessing Zotero While Reassessing Research." *Information Literacy: Research and Collaboration Across Disciplines*, edited by Barbara J. D'Angelo et al., The WAC Clearinghouse / University Press of Colorado, 2017, pp. 287–304, https://doi.org/10.37514/PER-B.2016.0834.2.14.

This second grouping contains works discussing online ABs (and related forms) that do not foreground pedagogical applications. The grouping is not comprehensive, but rather gives a sampling of how recent, online ABs and related forms are being conceptualized.

Barker, Elton, et al. "Coding for the Many, Transforming Knowledge for All: Annotating Digital Documents." *PMLA/Publications of the Modern Language Association of America*, vol. 135, no. 1, 2020, pp. 195–202, https://doi.org/10.1632/pmla.2020.135.1.195.

Kalir, Jeremiah H., and Jeremy Dean. "Web Annotation as Conversation and Interruption." *Media Practice and Education*, vol. 19, no. 1, 2018, pp. 18–29, https://doi.org/10.1080/14682753.2017.1362168.

Kalir, Remi, and Antero Garcia. *Annotation*. The MIT Press, 2021.

Muñoz, Caroline Lego. "More than Just Wikipedia: Creating a Collaborative Research Library Using a Wiki." *Marketing Education Review*, vol. 22, no. 1, 2012, pp. 21–26, https://doi.org/10.2753/MER1052-8008220104.

Novak, Elena, et al. "The Educational Use of Social Annotation Tools in Higher Education: A Literature Review." *The Internet and Higher Education*, vol. 15, no. 1, 2012, pp. 39–49, https://doi.org/10.1016/j.iheduc.2011.09.002.

Staines, Heather Ruland. "Digital Open Annotation with Hypothesis: Supplying the Missing Capability of the Web." *Journal of Scholarly Publishing*, vol. 49, no. 3, 2018, pp. 345–65, https://doi.org/10.3138/jsp.49.3.04.

3 Teaching Annotation Types

Cynthia A. Cochran and Luke Beatty

Annotation Types

For those who skipped "Chapter #1: History of the Annotated Bibliography" and "Chapter #2: The Annotated Bibliography in Higher Education," this chapter will get you up to speed on annotated bibliographies (ABs) and will introduce you to the five most common annotation types. For instructors and librarians looking for a quick grounding in ABs, this chapter will be a worthwhile read.

As the name suggests, an annotated bibliography combines a bibliography and an annotation. (A bibliography is an ordered list of references and an annotation is a note.) In an annotated bibliography, each entry has a corresponding annotation found below the reference in question. Annotations are typically written in full sentences that comment on a given source. The tenor and degree of detail in any one annotation, and the order of the bibliographic entries, will depend on the writer's purposes and context. See below for a sample AB entry:

> Emina, Seb. "In France, Comic Books Are Serious Business." *The New York Times*, 29 Jan. 2019, https://is.gd/KKGEUd
>
> This newspaper article, by Seb Emina, reports on France's annual *Angoulême International Comics Festival*. The author notes that by sales volume, most comics and graphic novels in the French/Belgian market are selling better than ever. Experts quoted in the article also suggest that the quality of these publications is higher than ever. This scene contrasts with the American market, where comic book and graphic novel sales tapered off as of 2018. Some information from this article will be useful as background/contextual material in my research, but I will also look for more updated figures.

For the purposes of AB assignments, undergraduates will typically write one of five different annotation types:

- Descriptive annotation – Identifies the main features and/or sections of a source.
- Summative annotation – Recaps the main points and/or arguments of a source.
- Evaluative annotation – Judges the credibility, reliability, and/or value of a source.
- Reflective annotation – Indicates how a source may be used in one's work or the field.
- Combined annotation – Incorporates two or more of the aforementioned annotation types.

Below, we discuss the particulars of each annotation type with examples and checklists. As you read, one thing to remember is that different disciplines prioritize different information, and so particular annotation types look different across different fields. If you assign an AB, be explicit about the kind of information the students should include in their annotations. Be similarly explicit about the writing style you expect.

Descriptive Annotations

A descriptive annotation identifies the main features and/or sections of a source. Descriptive annotations typically discuss a source's content, creator(s), format, and other notable details that capture the essence of a work. Ensure students write their descriptive annotations as if they were describing the source to an audience who is unfamiliar with the work. Your students should identify at least some of these commonly used points when writing their descriptive annotations, with the first three being most often included:

- Creators (e.g., authors, artists, organizations).
- Format (e.g., book, article, painting, website).
- Genre (e.g., historical study, literature review, experiment).
- Sections, chapters, bibliography, glossary, or other components.
- Special features (e.g., important tables, figures, diagrams).
- Intended audience and/or disciplinary field.
- Publisher.
- Length or size of the work.
- Anything else important for capturing the nature of the work.

Descriptive Annotation Example in MLA 9

Below you will find a model descriptive annotation written in the MLA 9 style for a paper on the Roman Games. Note that the discussion eschews critique and analysis in favor of simply listing the book section's content. A reasonably good student writer might produce such an annotation:

> Potter, David. "Part 4: Roman Games." *The Victor's Crown: A History of Ancient Sport from Homer to Byzantium*, Oxford University Press, 2012, pp. 163–222, https://is.gd/CJ17yT.
>
> This book section, entitled "Part 4: Roman Games," appears in David Potter's 2012 book, *The Victor's Crown: A History of Ancient Sport from Homer to Byzantium*. Potter is a professor of Greek and Roman history. The section contains five chapters: "Greece Meets Rome," wherein the influence of Greece on the Roman games is discussed; "Kings and Games," wherein the influence of high-ranking Roman officials on the Games is summarized; "Rome and Italy," wherein the influence of Italy on the Games is discussed; "Actors and Gladiators," wherein the actors and gladiators are discussed; and "Caesar, Antony, Augustus" and the Games, wherein the influence of political figures on the Games is analyzed. Potter includes select illustrations, photographs, and extensive notes throughout.

Descriptive Annotation Checklist

Below you will find a checklist you can use to remind students about a descriptive annotation's key features:

Descriptive Annotation Checklist

- Who are the source's authors or creators?
    - What are their credentials?
        - Hint: Check for an author biographical statement near the beginning or end of the source.
- What is the format of the source (e.g., book, article, website)?
    - Is it a popular, academic, commercial, professional, or governmental source?
    - Is it peer-reviewed?
        - Hint: Check with the library or the sponsoring organization's website to see if the source is peer-reviewed.
- What is the genre of the source (e.g., historical narrative, sculpture, scholarly article)?
- When was the source created or published?
- What type of material is used in the source (including artistic materials)?
- What are the main components of the source (write as if to an audience who has no access to the work)?
    - For books, what are the sections or chapters?
    - For articles, what are the section headings?
    - For websites, what are the webpages?
    - Does it have a bibliography?
    - Does it have a glossary, table of contents, index, or appendix?
    - For works of art, what type of material is used to make the art?
- Are there special features in the source, such as tables, figures, charts, images, and so on?
- Who is the intended audience?
- Who published the source (e.g., company, individual, some person on the Internet)?
- What is the length/size of the source?
- Are there other important factors you should note in order to adequately describe the source?

Summative Annotations

A summative annotation condenses key points or arguments in a source. Summative annotations typically require an opening sentence describing the source's format and creator. That sentence is then followed by a recap of the source's purpose, thesis, and main points. While a descriptive annotation lists a work's content, a summative annotation actually unpacks the work itself. Ensure students write their summative annotations as if they were summarizing the source to an audience who is unfamiliar with the work. Your students should identify at least some of these commonly used points when writing their summative annotations:

- [elements necessary for all annotations] Creators (e.g., authors, artists, organizations).
- [elements necessary for all annotations] Format (e.g., book, article, website).
- Main or key themes of the work.
- The purpose, thesis, or hypothesis of the work (if applicable).
- Argument(s) and rebuttal(s), if present.
- Theories, perspectives, lenses, or styles governing the work.

Summative Annotation Example in MLA 9

Below, you will find a model summative annotation written in the MLA 9 style for a paper on the Roman Games. Note that the first two sentences are primarily descriptive, which helps contextualize the summative annotation (or annotations of any type, really). A reasonably good student writer might produce such an annotation:

Potter, David. "Part 4: Roman Games." *The Victor's Crown: A History of Ancient Sport from Homer to Byzantium*, Oxford University Press, 2012, pp. 163–222, https://is.gd/CJ17yT.

This book section, entitled "Part 4: Roman Games," is found in David Potter's book *The Victor's Crown: A History of Ancient Sport from Homer to Byzantium*. The section includes five chapters in which Potter discusses the Roman Games, circa 300 BCE-100 AD. Potter touches on activities performed in the Games, including boxing, wrestling, chariot racing, and gladiatorial combat. He also discusses some of the athletes in the Games, including members of the ruling class. In this section, Potter is particularly interested in examining the symbolic and political value of the Games, arguing that rulers used the Games to advance regime goals and their own political ends. Finally, he traces the influence of neighboring states, particularly Greece and Italy, on the Games.

Summative Annotation Checklist

Below, you will find a checklist you can use to remind students about a summative annotation's key features:

Summative Annotation Checklist

- ❏ What is the subject of the work?
- ❏ What is the work's purpose – to argue/evaluate, explain/inform, or entertain?
- ❏ What is the main thrust of the work (explain it as if to an audience who has not read the work)?
  - ❏ For nonfiction books, what is the thesis or main point?
  - ❏ For scientific studies, what is the problem, research question, and hypothesis? What are the methods, analyses, findings, and conclusions?
  - ❏ For arguments, what are the major claims, objections, and rebuttals?
  - ❏ For explanatory or informative sources, what is explained?
- ❏ If the work is written to respond to a problem, what is the problem?
- ❏ For fiction:
  - ❏ What is the setting and theme?
  - ❏ Who are the main characters?
  - ❏ What are the main events in the plot?
  - ❏ What are important symbols (if any)?
  - ❏ What is the climax?
- ❏ For other creative works, what are the main components of the work (e.g., the main symbols in a poem or a painting)?
- ❏ Are there any crucial facts, definitions, or quotations that help capture the essence of the work?
- ❏ What information can you safely omit from your annotation?

Evaluative Annotations

An evaluative annotation (sometimes referred to as a "critical annotation") critiques or judges the worthiness of a source. The evaluative annotation should begin with an opening sentence describing the source's format and creator. Following that, the evaluative annotation may praise, condemn, appreciate, or express indifference toward a work. A critique may take many forms but can include judgments about how convincing a work is; the coherence, factuality, or comprehensiveness of the work; the currency of the work; readability; creativity; value of the work to a community; and the credibility of the work's creator or publisher. When writing evaluative annotations, your students should consider at least some of the following:

- [elements necessary for all annotations] Creators (e.g., authors, artists, organizations).
- [elements necessary for all annotations] Format (e.g., book, article, website).
- Factuality.
- Convincingness of argument(s) or idea(s) presented in the source.
- Readability (for written works) or coherence.
- Creativity.
- Comprehensiveness.
- Value of the source to a given community.
- Credibility of the creator(s) or publisher.
- Currency of the source.

Evaluative Annotation Example in MLA 9

Below, you will find a model evaluative annotation written in the MLA 9 style for a paper on the Roman Games. Note that the first two sentences are primarily descriptive, which helps contextualize the evaluative annotation (or annotations of any type, really). The subsequent sentences then assess the value of Potter's work and his evidence. A reasonably good student writer might produce such an annotation:

Potter, David. "Part 4: Roman Games." *The Victor's Crown: A History of Ancient Sport from Homer to Byzantium*, Oxford University Press, 2012, pp. 163–222, https://is.gd/CJ17yT.

This book section, entitled "Part 4: Roman Games," is found in David Potter's book *The Victor's Crown: A History of Ancient Sport from Homer to Byzantium*. The section includes five chapters discussing aspects of the Roman Games, circa 300 BCE-100 AD. Taken as a whole, the chapters provide a reasonable overview of the activities, athletes, venues, and spectators involved with the Games. However, Potter is most interested in the symbolic and political value of the Games. Potter argues that the Games provided a unique venue for Roman dignitaries to flaunt their wealth, bolster their popular support, and heighten their reputations. Ultimately, these displays of political dominance boosted their standing in high society. The evidence for these claims is extensive and persuasive, and by discussing the political context of the Games, Potter provides a unique lens of analysis.

Evaluative Annotation Checklist

Below, you will find a checklist you can use to remind students about an evaluative annotation's key features:

Evaluative Annotation Checklist

- Consider the content of the source in terms of its value:
  - For argumentative works, how logical is the argument?
    - Does the conclusion follow from the premise?
    - Are important counter-arguments fairly addressed?
    - Does the analysis seem reasonable?
- How factual is the source (if applicable)? Is it up to date?
- How comprehensive is the source?
- How valid and reliable are the research findings?
- How important are the conclusions to the discipline or to other relevant communities?
- For creative works, how well does the work stand up to aesthetic judgment or disciplinary principles? How original is it?
- How would you rate the method(s) used in the work?
  - To what extent are the methods appropriate to the subject?
  - Are the methods carried out well?
- How trustworthy is the author or publisher? Is the author or publisher known for expertise or credibility?
- How coherent is the work? For written works, how would you evaluate the prose?

Reflective Annotations

A reflective annotation tells how and in what context one plans to use a source (or how others might use it). This reflection connects one's knowledge of a source to one's research goals. The reflective annotation typically begins with an opening sentence describing a source's format and creator. This is followed by a discussion of how the writer plans to use the source. A useful reflective annotation recognizes that "good," "bad," and "mediocre" sources can all be useful in different contexts. When teaching the reflective annotation, you should remind students that a source's value is contextual and that some of the following elements should be discussed in their reflective annotations:

- [elements necessary for all annotations] Creators (e.g., authors, artists, organizations).
- [elements necessary for all annotations] Format (e.g., book, article, website).
- How the source contributes to a research plan.
- How or where particular sections of the source will be used.
- How the source connects to other sources.
- How "bad" or "mediocre" sources might still have value to the writer.
- How theories, perspectives, lenses, or styles in the source connect with the writer's agenda.

Reflective Annotation Example in MLA 9

Below, you will find a model reflective annotation written in the MLA 9 style for a paper on the Roman Games. Note that the first two sentences are primarily descriptive, which helps contextualize the reflective annotation (or annotations of any type, really). The subsequent sentences link the section's content to writer's research plan. A reasonably good student writer might produce such an annotation:

Potter, David. "Part 4: Roman Games." *The Victor's Crown: A History of Ancient Sport from Homer to Byzantium*, Oxford University Press, 2012, pp. 163–222, https://is.gd/CJ17yT.

This book section, entitled "Part 4: Roman Games," appears in David Potter's 2012 book. The section includes five chapters discussing aspects of the Roman Games, circa 300 BCE-100 AD. Potter addresses many aspects of the Games that will help me write my paper, though his section on the Games' venues will be especially useful. Potter also stresses the political and symbolic value of the Games, and because most of my research delves into the nuts and bolts of particular sports (e.g., rules, equipment, venues, etc.), Potter's section provides me with excellent contextual material to support my argument.

Reflective Annotation Checklist

Below, you will find a checklist you can use to remind students about a reflective annotation's key features:

Reflective Annotation Checklist

- ❏ Is this source relevant to your research? Does it fit with your research plan?
- ❏ Is the source a major or minor contributor to your research needs?
  - ❏ For argumentative works, how and where would you use the major claims, evidence, or counterclaims in your paper?
  - ❏ For informative works, how and where would the examples, explanations, facts, or definitions fit in your paper?
  - ❏ For creative works, how and where might you refer to important concepts or examples from the work, such as a description of the work itself, individual parts or scenes, or how the work relates to other works of its kind, and so on.
- ❏ Is the method used in the work one that you might replicate, explain, or criticize in your paper?
- ❏ If you plan to use a "bad" or "mediocre" source, explain why you are using it (e.g., as a counter-example).
- ❏ Does this source "fit" with your other research?
  - ❏ Does this source fill a gap? If so, how?
  - ❏ Does this source agree or disagree with other sources? If so, how?
- ❏ Do other works by the author/creator look useful? Do works listed in the source's bibliography look useful to you?

Combined Annotations

A combined annotation uses some or all of the previously described annotation types (descriptive, summative, evaluative, and reflective). A combined annotation should begin with a descriptive sentence naming the author(s) and format of the source, followed by a short summary of the main purpose or argument(s) of the source. Subsequent to that, a combined annotation can include as much descriptive, summative, evaluative, or reflective commentary as the writer deems necessary. Students obliged to give lengthier treatments of their work should use combined annotations, and would do well to consider including some (but not all!) of the following elements:

- [elements necessary for all annotations] Creators (e.g., authors, artists, organizations).
- [elements necessary for all annotations] Format (e.g., book, article, website).
- Genre (e.g., historical study, literature review, experiment).
- Sections, chapters, bibliography, glossary, or other components.
- Special features (e.g., important tables, figures, diagrams).
- Intended audience and/or disciplinary field.
- Publisher.
- Length or size of the work.
- Anything else important for capturing the nature of the work.
- Main or key themes of the work.
- The purpose, thesis, or hypothesis of the work (if applicable).
- Argument(s) and rebuttal(s), if present.
- Theories, perspectives, lenses, or styles governing the work.
- Factuality.
- Convincingness of argument(s) or idea(s) presented in the source.
- Readability (for written works) or coherence.
- Creativity.
- Comprehensiveness.
- Value of the source to a given community.
- Credibility of the creator(s) or publisher.
- Currency of the source.
- How the source contributes to a research plan.
- How or where particular sections of the source will be used.
- How the source connects to other sources.
- How "bad" or "mediocre" sources might still have value to the writer.
- How theories, perspectives, lenses, or styles in the source connect with the writer's agenda.

Combined Annotation Example in MLA 9

Below, you will find a model combined annotation written in the MLA 9 style for a paper on the Roman Games. Though this annotation is shorter than a typical combined annotation would be, note that it describes, summarizes, evaluates, and briefly reflects on the source. A reasonably good student writer might produce such an annotation:

> Potter, David. "Part 4: Roman Games." *The Victor's Crown: A History of Ancient Sport from Homer to Byzantium*, Oxford University Press, 2012, pp. 163–222, https://is.gd/CJ17yT.
>
> This book section, entitled "Part 4: Roman Games," appears in David Potter's 2012 book *The Victor's Crown: A History of Ancient Sport from Homer to Byzantium*. The section includes five chapters discussing aspects of the Roman Games, circa 300 BCE-100 AD. Potter highlights activities performed in the Games, including boxing, wrestling, chariot racing, and gladiatorial combat. He also discusses some of the athletes in the Games, including members of the ruling class. Potter is particularly interested, however, in unpacking the symbolic and political value of the Games, arguing that rulers used the Games to advance regime goals and their own political ends.
>
> The chapters provide a reasonable overview of the activities, athletes, venues, and spectators who frequented the Games. However, Potter's interest in the symbolic and political value of the Games most interests me. I am especially taken with Potter's argument that the Games provided a unique venue for Roman dignitaries to flaunt their wealth, bolster their popular support, and heighten their reputation. Potter's emphasis on the political dimensions of the Games will provide me with excellent contextual material to support my research. I will not use many of Potter's other details, however.

Combined Annotation Checklist

Below, you will find a checklist you can use to remind students about a combined annotation's key features:

Combined Annotation Checklist

- ❏ How detailed does your description need to be (given a reader who has no access to the work)?
    - ❏ Have you identified the author and source format?
    - ❏ Is the source popular, scholarly, or peer-reviewed?
    - ❏ Do you need to further describe the source?
- ❏ To what degree do you need to summarize the source (given an audience who has not read the work)?
    - ❏ Besides the main thesis and purpose (which you should include no matter what), do you need to add supporting details?
    - ❏ For argumentative sources, have you adequately captured the main line of reasoning which supports the conclusion?
    - ❏ Are there any details, facts, definitions, or quotes you want to include?
- ❏ To what extent do you need to evaluate the source?
    - ❏ Is there something important about the author or publisher that affects the work's credibility?
    - ❏ Is there anything about the content, argument, or conclusion you would like to praise or condemn?
    - ❏ Have you evaluated the author's methods? Are they appropriate and carried out well?
- ❏ What can you say as you reflect upon the utility of the source?
    - ❏ How and/or where might you use it in your research?
    - ❏ If it is a "bad" or "mediocre" source, is there a good way to use it?
    - ❏ Have you reflected on how this source fits with other sources you have found?
- ❏ Do any annotations need to go into more depth given the source and the topic?
- ❏ Have you used the other four annotation type checklists to guide you?

Further Reading

Beatty, Luke, and Cynthia A. Cochran. *Writing the Annotated Bibliography: A Guide for Students and Researchers.* Routledge, 2020, https://doi.org/10.4324/9780367853051.

Eula, Michael J., and Janet Madden. *Compiling the Annotated Bibliography: A Guide.* 2nd ed., Kendall/Hunt Publishing Company, 1995.

Harner, James L. *On Compiling an Annotated Bibliography.* 2nd ed., Modern Language Association of America, 2000.

4 Assignments for Composition and WAC Classes

Cynthia A. Cochran

Introduction

The annotated bibliography (AB) is an increasingly important component of composition and other courses, but many students – especially first-year undergraduates – have no experience writing ABs. Likewise, instructors may be used to writing ABs but new to teaching students how to do so.

This chapter offers easily adapted AB assignments for composition and writing across the curriculum (WAC) classes. The first three assignments are especially relevant for developmental composition courses or the first course in a two-semester composition sequence. Some lessons are easily modified for upper-level composition, graduate, or even high school courses. Several assignments can be sequenced to scaffold students' learning experiences. The chapter ends with a further reading section.

Each assignment in this chapter is inspired by examples from professional literature and my experience. For constancy, most assignments are laid out in a fixed template, outlined as follows:

- Timeline – How long the assignment should take from rollout to submission.
- Audience – Courses/students that would benefit most from the assignment.
- Activity Description – an explanation of the scope and sequence of assignment activities.
- Learning Outcome(s) – What students are expected to learn from the assignment.
- Teaching Notes – Some advice on teaching the assignment and things to watch out for.
- Variants – Some variations on the base assignment.
- Assignment Sheet – Instructions for the assignment.
- Rubric – Assessment tool for evaluating the assignment.

DOI: 10.4324/9781003214434-4

Assignments for Composition and WAC Classes 43

All assignments in this chapter align with the standards listed below:

Organization	Standards Alignment
Council of Writing Programs and the National Council of Teachers of English: WPA Outcomes for First-Year Composition (3.0)	Critical Thinking, Reading, and Composing, especially these outcomes: • Use composing and reading for inquiry, learning, critical thinking, and communicating in various rhetorical contexts. • Read a diverse range of texts, attending especially to relationships between assertion and evidence, to patterns of organization, to the interplay between verbal and nonverbal elements, and to how these features function for different audiences and situations. • Locate and evaluate (for credibility, sufficiency, accuracy, timeliness, bias, and so on) primary and secondary research materials, including journal articles and essays, books, scholarly and professionally established and maintained databases or archives, and informal electronic networks and Internet sources. Processes, especially Knowledge of Conventions: • Learn common formats and/or design features for different kinds of texts. • Explore the concepts of intellectual property (such as fair use and copyright) that motivate documentation conventions. • Practice applying citation conventions systematically in their own work.
Common Core English Language Arts (ELA)	Grades 11–12 ELA Standards 1, 2, 4, 6, 7, and 8.

Preliminary Notes on Instruction

The advice in this section applies to all the assignments in the chapter. Before reviewing the assignments, I recommend reading this section first.

If you are teaching first-year students, know that they will probably be unfamiliar with ABs and may be unaware of how to conduct college-level research. Depending on the assignment and the students' background experience, you will need to prepare lessons or work with a librarian to cover basics of selecting a topic; citing sources; formatting and organizing an AB; creating the five types of annotations; finding appropriate sources; and using an AB to plan/outline and draft a follow-up paper.

Many assignments, especially those asking students to find high-quality sources, may best be paired with an information literacy (IL) course taught by a librarian. In any case, if you need to prepare students to accurately cite sources, my advice is to introduce them to a plug-and-play citation generation service (see https://library.ic.edu/cite for options). Because many citation generators make mistakes – and all of them spit back only what students input – let students know that the full suite of rules governing any given documentation system is listed in many style manuals and handbooks. If the library has in-house citation guides, you might also introduce those options to clean up any citations produced by a citation generation service.

If you work with a librarian, my advice is that for each IL lesson you collaborate on, students should contribute additional sources to their ABs. For example, if an IL class is devoted to finding books, students should be expected to find books for their AB. You may decide for various reasons not to collaborate with a librarian, especially if your composition instruction includes lessons on finding and citing appropriate sources, if students are limited to selected curated databases, or if you are working with students who are already comfortable using library resources.

Some assignments assume a deficit of prior research experience on the students' parts. It is probably best to assume that the majority of first-year students will be unfamiliar with ABs and that most will be ignorant of how to conduct and write up college-level research. AB assignments can act as low-stakes launching pads for developing students – students can learn a little about the kinds of sources they need to find, how to cite and evaluate those sources, how to format the AB, how to write annotations, and potentially how to use their AB in composing a follow-up paper.

All assignments in this chapter have a tailored rubric. Feel free to use rubrics for educational, non-commercial purposes. For notes on teaching the five annotation types, see "Chapter #3: Teaching Annotation Types." For tips on how to help students annotate common sources, see "Chapter #8: Teaching Source Types." For reproducible model ABs, see "Chapter #9: Three Sample Annotated Bibliographies."

Accessibility: you should take the special needs of your students into consideration by applying principles of universal design (UD) in your teaching. For example, students with visual impairment may need assistive reading devices. As another example, students who are deaf or hard of hearing can learn more easily if an AB assignment is presented visually. Principles of UD can assist you by providing ideas about how to adapt lessons for students with special needs, with an abundance of articles, websites, and YouTube videos to help. Although a fulsome discussion of UD is beyond the scope of this chapter, one place to start is Nielsen's article on teaching composition with UD in mind.

Assignment #1: Basic Annotation Skills

This assignment introduces students to the concepts of bibliographic citation and annotation (especially descriptive and summative annotations) and to the general format of ABs created with a set of assigned sources. The assignment introduces students to mechanics of describing and summarizing common types of sources such as book chapters, scholarly/popular articles, or webpages.

Audience

Developmental composition classes or the first of a two-course composition sequence.

Timeline

Two to three weeks. The depth of instruction needed and the number of sources students must annotate will affect the assignment timeline.

Learning Outcomes / Students Will...

- Produce a properly formatted AB (typically alphabetized).
- Produce reasonably correct bibliographic citations.
- Clearly articulate a topic and thesis in an introductory paragraph.
- Annotate a small number of sources in a manner consistent with assignment specifications, for example, with descriptive, summative, or free-form annotations.

Activity Description

In this assignment, students will produce a short AB, with perhaps three sources. The AB will include an introductory paragraph that specifies the topic and a working thesis. Sources may be cited in whichever style is prevalent in the course. In their annotations, students will focus on describing and summarizing sources that are provided for them and that are familiar to the instructor. In this case, library instruction is unnecessary except, perhaps, that which focuses on source type and citation. Teaching these two concepts together helps students learn to write a correct citation and good annotation for each source.

Alternatively, if students are required to find their own sources or to add a source to those given to them, the assignment may be paired with more robust IL instruction addressing the mechanics of finding library sources.

Concepts introduced in this assignment will be new to most developmental writers, so this assignment focuses on descriptive and summative annotations. It prescribes a length requirement of four to six sentences to guide students and is evaluated on writing quality and correct citations. The main objective is to get students to create an AB by composing an introductory paragraph with a topic and working thesis; crafting proper citations; writing and organizing annotations to describe and summarize sources accurately, clearly, and without plagiarism; and organizing the AB entries.

Students may become more motivated if they can respond to the sources; doing so allows them to articulate their opinions and affords them a rhetorical purpose. You can have them write their opinions in a separate paragraph or write a follow-up summary-response paper, keeping these separate from the annotations so as to ascertain the students' ability to summarize texts more or less objectively.

Teaching Notes

To optimize student success on this assignment, you can curate a list of sources for topics of interest to students, and it may be motivating for them to be able to choose from among several topics. By being familiar with the sources, you can more easily gauge whether students have accurately described and summarized them.

This is likely the first, or one of the first, research writing assignments for students, so prepare instructions on correctly identifying source types and citing sources. If students use a citation generator, warn them about the mistakes that such generators can make even when correct information is typed in.

You will also need to provide instruction on how to build and format ABs and, most crucially, on how to write descriptive and summative annotations. In grading, you can gently remind students that in the future they will be expected to use an increasing variety of academic sources, but herein they are building basic skills.

Of course, students will be curious about what to write in their annotations. Subsequent assignments in this chapter prescribe the writing of other types of annotations, but this assignment is focused on the basic skills of describing and summarizing sources accurately and clearly. You may wish to assure students that their focus should be on accurate, clear, and original writing. Students will need instruction on what makes a good descriptive annotation, but perhaps more crucially, lower-level students will almost certainly need instruction in writing summative annotations. For example, their initial summaries may suffer from being overly broad or list-like, or from failing to capture a source's main line of argument.

It may be helpful to instruct students on using sentence beginnings and transitions, such as "According to . . . " and "The authors add that . . . ," to achieve coherence in their writing and to signal that they are reporting on a source rather than writing about their own ideas. This practice prepares them for more success in writing research papers. Other advice:

- Ensure students create their AB in tandem with your instruction. After each class/lesson, prompt students to contribute something to their AB, be it an introductory paragraph, correct citations, a working thesis, or an annotation. Keep them working!
- Do not underestimate the difficulty students have in formatting their ABs. Provide them an editable template in the relevant format.
- Spend sufficient time going over an AB's form, its main components, and its purpose. Though students will run into ABs throughout their academic careers, this might be the first one they see, so ensure they are comfortable with the form.
- Instruct students on the types of annotation you wish them to produce.
- Be clear about whether/how you want them to name authors or use quotes in the annotations.
- You may need to explain why copying an abstract, even from a database, constitutes plagiarism.
- You may need lessons on summarizing and paraphrasing accurately.
- Providing choice among several topics and curated lists can be motivating. Consider adding a new choice each semester in which you use this assignment.

Variants

- Students may be asked to add one source to a set of assigned sources.
- Students may be asked to write a paper comparing the sources.

- Students may be asked to write a follow-up summary-response paper or a mini-research paper.
- For collaborative writing, the class may be given a common topic. Individuals or groups may have a subset of sources related to that topic and then asked to contribute their annotations to a small-group or whole-class bibliography.

Basic Annotation Skills Instructions

Overview: In this assignment, you will create a [#-source] annotated bibliography (AB) on a topic you select from several options and sources that are given to you. Over the next [# weeks] you will complete your AB bit by bit, and you will have the chance to incorporate feedback and revisions before submitting your complete AB. This assignment is worth [%] of your course grade. [You will not write a follow-up research paper, so the AB itself is your paper.]
What is an Annotated Bibliography? A "bibliography" is an ordered list of sources – books, articles, websites, and so on – to which you refer in your work. An "annotation" is a note to describe, summarize, evaluate, and/or reflect on a source. Thus, an "annotated bibliography" is an ordered list of reference citations, each one followed by an annotation.
Purpose of the Assignment: This assignment will prepare you for more extensive research writing.
Specific Requirements for AB:

- It will be on a topic assigned to you [with sources provided].
- It will contain an introductory paragraph, which will briefly describe the research topic and contain a working thesis (as if you were going to write a research paper on the topic).
- It will contain [#] sources that will be provided to you [with # additional source that you find].
- It will follow the formatting guidelines we discuss in class and which you find modeled in the sample AB at the end of this assignment sheet.
- Each source will be cited in the [MLA] style, and the sources will be alphabetized.

- For each source, you will write an annotation that describes the source (tells the kind of source it is, such as a 20-page book chapter or a 6-page peer-reviewed research article) and that summarizes the source's main points and argument.
- Each annotation will be between [4–6] sentences. We will discuss strategies for writing a good annotation in class.
- Do not quote in the annotation. Instead, reword ideas in your own style.

Audience: Another researcher. Assume your reader has a working knowledge of your topic and wants to learn more. Don't assume, however, that the reader has an insider's knowledge.

Rhetorical Purpose: To record and inform.

Assumptions: When you write your annotations, you are researching the particular thesis from your introduction ("Youth should devote one year of service before college" or "Superman would beat Batman"). Thus, you can select main points that are most significant for your thesis!

[**Sample Annotated Bibliography:** It helps students if you include a sample AB with their assignment. See "Chapter #9: Three Sample Annotated Bibliographies" for sample ABs.]

Basic Annotation Skills Rubric

	Proficient	Competent	Developing	Inadequate
Introductory Paragraph	Introductory paragraph has the topic and thesis specified. Text is proficiently written.	Introductory paragraph has the topic and thesis specified. Text is competently written.	Introductory paragraph has the topic and thesis specified. Text is indifferently written.	Introductory paragraph is absent, unclear, or does not articulate a topic or thesis.
Overall Annotation Writing Quality	Annotations conform to specified length, are well-written, grammatically sound, and fully capture the essence of sources.	Annotations conform to specified length, are mostly well-written, and adequately capture the essence of sources.	Annotations conform to specified length, are largely coherent, and somewhat capture the essence of sources.	Annotations do not conform to specified length, are incoherent, or inadequately capture the essence of sources.
Descriptive Annotation Quality	All annotations contain one or more phrases to accurately describe the sources.	Most annotations contain one or more phrases to accurately describe the sources, but one description is inaccurate.	Two or more annotations contain phrases to describe sources, but two descriptions are missing or inaccurate.	The descriptions are generally inaccurate or missing.

(Continued)

	Proficient	Competent	Developing	Inadequate
Summative Annotation Quality	All summaries are accurate, include the main points and purposes of the sources, and are well paraphrased.	Most summaries are accurate, include the main points and purposes of the sources, but are not all well paraphrased.	Two or more summaries have problems with accuracy, completeness, or improper paraphrasing.	Most or all summaries are inaccurate, incomplete, or improperly paraphrased.
Citations	Citations are entirely error-free. Formatting is correct.	Citations contain very few errors. Formatting is correct.	Citations contain some errors. Formatting is mostly correct.	Citations are absent or contain frequent errors. Formatting is incorrect.
Overall Formatting	Properly alphabetized AB conforms to assignment formatting requirements with no errors.	Properly alphabetized AB conforms to assignment formatting requirements with only 1–2 errors.	Alphabetized AB conforms to assignment formatting requirements with occasional errors.	AB is improperly alphabetized and fails to conform to assignment formatting requirements, or has many errors.

Any AB containing plagiarized material will be returned with a grade of zero (0) and appropriate steps will be taken.

Assignment #2: Preliminary Annotated Bibliography

The Preliminary Annotated Bibliography assignment eases students into library research, bibliographic citation, annotation, and ABs by affording them a "storage bin" to house research as they practice mechanics of finding sources and annotating them. It may be done as a follow-up to Assignment #1, as a prelude to any assignment from this chapter, or as the first step in any research paper unit.

Audience

Either developmental writing students, other composition students, or students in WAC courses with a research paper component. Developing writers are introduced to college-level research and students in other composition or WAC courses can use this assignment as the first step in a longer research project.

Timeline

Two to four weeks. The depth of instruction needed and the number of sources students must find and annotate will affect the timeline.

Learning Outcomes / Students Will...

- Locate a minimum number of appropriate research sources.
- Produce a properly formatted AB (typically alphabetized).
- Produce reasonably correct bibliographic citations.
- Clearly articulate a topic, researchable question, and thesis in an introductory paragraph.
- Annotate a set number of research sources with any cogent comment they deem appropriate, or by using one or more of the five annotation types.
- Use the preliminary AB to alter their research focus if necessary.

Activity Description

In this assignment, students will find sources and produce a preliminary AB. The AB will have an introductory paragraph that outlines the student's topic, states the research question, and includes a working thesis. Sources may be cited in whichever style the course uses.

Because many concepts introduced in this assignment may be new to first-year undergraduates, I do not prescribe particular requirements for the annotations themselves beyond length and clear, well-edited writing. However, I recommend that students describe the source by at least identifying the type (e.g., popular magazine article vs. academic journal article) since they will need to know the types in order to create proper citations. In addition, they will have better outcomes on their papers if they are also asked to include an evaluative annotation. A length requirement of, say, 4–6 sentences will help guide students' writing. The real objective, though, is to get students to create a preliminary AB by crafting proper citations, writing annotations as a form of taking research notes, composing a good introductory paragraph, and organizing AB entries in a useful manner. This is ultimately done in the service of preparing to write a research paper.

Teaching Notes

To optimize student success, prepare lessons or work with a librarian to cover the basics of topic selection, resource location, and citation, if not also source evaluation. You will also need to develop lessons on how to build ABs (including explicit instruction about formatting them) and on what you expect of the annotations.

This assignment can work with popular or academic sources. Developmental writers may be more comfortable if they can work with popular sources, allowing instruction to focus more on the fundamentals of research and AB formation. In grading, you can gently remind developmental students that in the future they will need to use an increasing number of academic sources, but for the moment they are building basic skills. Other students will find this assignment useful in their first step in a research project.

Even students who have already done some research writing or who use a citation generator will need reinforcement on how to accurately cite sources. Ultimately, though, the goal for the search/citation dimensions of the assignment should be to have students locate appropriate sources, correctly identify source types, generate a reasonable citation for each source, and get their research started!

Lastly, students will vary in their initial ability to write useful annotations. Subsequent assignments in this chapter prescribe certain approaches to writing annotations, but this assignment is quite relaxed about how students write them. Assure students that their focus should be on clear and thoughtful writing and that all entries should contain a basic description of the type and nature of the source. Summative annotations can be brief if this assignment is used before students revise and expand their annotations for a more formal AB. Free-form annotations may be best in a developmental course. For advanced students, the evaluative annotation will prove most useful at this juncture.

Important notes on teaching include the following:

- Students are most likely being asked to write a follow-up research paper, in which case more attention needs to be paid to topic selection and thesis statements.
- You may wish to approve sources before students annotate too vigorously.
- Ensure students create their AB in tandem with your instruction. After each class/lesson, prompt students to contribute something to their AB.
- Consider providing students a template – either in *Microsoft Word* or *Google Docs* – that they can use to guide their formatting.
- Ensure you spend sufficient time going over what an AB is, what its elements are, and why you are using it as an assignment in your course. Though students will encounter ABs throughout their academic careers, this might be the first one they see, so ensure they are comfortable.
- Instruct students on the type(s) of annotation you wish them to produce.
- Expect brief annotations.
- Students may need a reminder that copying an abstract, even from a database, constitutes plagiarism.
- Note that evaluative annotations are sometimes referred to as "critical annotations."

Variants

- Students may be assigned one or more sources to get them off the ground.
- If the assignment follows Assignment #1, students may be asked to find and annotate additional sources as well as add evaluative and reflective annotations to their earlier AB. This variation works well if students are following up their ABs by writing a research paper.

- Students may be asked to find their sources exclusively from a particular database.
- Students may be asked to include a combination of popular and academic sources.
- Students may be asked to write a paper comparing their sources.

Preliminary Annotated Bibliography Instructions

Overview: You will create a [#-source] preliminary annotated bibliography (AB) on a research topic of your choice, approved by me. Over the next [# weeks] you will find and annotate sources, incorporate feedback, and revise [before submitting a complete AB]. This assignment is worth [%] of the course grade. [You will/will not write a follow-up research paper with its own grade.]

What is a Preliminary Annotated Bibliography? "Preliminary," of course, means first. A "bibliography" is an ordered list of sources – books, articles, websites, and so on – to which you refer in your work. An "annotation" is a note that is usually written to describe, summarize, evaluate, and/or reflect on a source. Thus, a "preliminary bibliography" is an ordered list of citations, each one followed by an annotation, used to explore a research topic.

Purpose of the Assignment: This assignment will prepare you for writing a research paper.

Specific Requirements for AB:

- It will be on a topic of your choice that I must approve in [week #].
- It will contain an introductory paragraph, which will briefly discuss why you picked the topic, tell what you hope to learn (in the form of a research question), and include a specific and focused working thesis appropriate for a research paper that uses the sources.
- It will contain [#] reputable sources.
- It will follow the formatting guidelines we discuss in class and which you find modeled in the sample AB at the end of this assignment sheet.
- Each source will be cited in the [MLA] style, and the sources will be alphabetized.

- For each source you will write a brief annotation of [#–#] complete sentences.
- The annotation will be placed immediately after its source citation. In each annotation, you will describe the source (e.g., is it a book, a scholarly journal article, a page from a website? Is it scholarly or popular? Is it peer-reviewed?); capture the essence of the source; and make your comments on whatever interests you about the source. In class, we will discuss some strategies for writing a good annotation.

Audience: You, and me as your instructor. Assume I have a working knowledge of your topic and want to learn more.
Rhetorical Purpose: To record and inform.
Assumptions: When you write your annotations, you are researching the thesis from your introductory paragraph (e.g., "Youth should devote one year of service before college" or "Superman would beat Batman in battle"). You may revise your thesis before the final draft of your AB!
[**Sample Annotated Bibliography:** It helps students if you include a sample AB with their assignment. See "Chapter #9: Three Sample Annotated Bibliographies" for sample ABs].

Preliminary Annotated Bibliography Rubric

	Proficient	Competent	Developing	Inadequate
Introductory Paragraph	Introductory paragraph is present. Text is proficiently written, and the research question and thesis are well-formulated.	Introductory paragraph is present. Text is competently written, and the research question and thesis are well-formulated.	Introductory paragraph is present. Text is indifferently written, and the research question or thesis is vague or overly broad.	Introductory paragraph is absent, unclear, or does not articulate a research question or research interest, or the thesis is missing.
Source Quality	Found correct number and type of sources. Sources highly related to the topic and display considerable expertise.	Found correct number and type of sources. Sources related to the topic, with most displaying at least a respectable level of expertise.	Found correct number and type of sources. Sources related to the topic, though may lack a degree of expertise (e.g., none from the library or its database).	Did not find correct number or type of sources. Sources are irrelevant or only loosely related to the topic.
Overall Annotation Writing Quality	Annotations conform to specified length. Annotations are well-written, grammatically sound, and fully capture the essence of sources.	Annotations conform to specified length. Annotations are well-written and adequately capture the essence of sources.	Annotations conform to specified length. Annotations are largely coherent and somewhat capture the essence of sources.	Annotations do not conform to specified length. Annotations are incoherent or inadequately capture the essence of sources.

Descriptive Annotation Quality	All annotations contain one or more phrases to accurately describe the type and nature of the sources.	All annotations contain one or more phrases to describe the type and nature of the sources, but some are inaccurate.	Most annotations contain one or more phrases to describe the type and nature of the sources, but some descriptions are missing or are not accurate.	Few or no annotation contains any phrases to accurately describe the type and nature of the sources, or descriptions are generally inaccurate.
Citations	Citations are entirely error-free. Formatting is correct.	Citations contain very few errors. Formatting is correct.	Citations contain some errors. Formatting is mostly correct.	Citations are absent or contain frequent errors. Formatting is incorrect.
AB Formatting	AB is correctly alphabetized, and the formatting conforms to assignment requirements with no errors.	AB is correctly alphabetized, and the formatting largely conforms to assignment requirements with only 1–2 errors.	AB is generally correctly alphabetized, and the formatting largely conforms to assignment requirements with occasional errors.	AB is not correctly alphabetized, or the formatting does not conform to assignment requirements or is largely incorrect.

Any AB containing plagiarized material will be returned with a grade of zero (0) and appropriate steps will be taken.

Assignment #3: Complete Annotated Bibliography

The Complete Annotated Bibliography assignment serves to engage students in research by having them revise and expand a more loosely written preliminary AB, or create a fully developed AB from scratch, by using the five types of annotation (descriptive, summative, evaluative, reflective, and combined). It may be assigned with or without a follow-up research paper. This assignment can be used in place of Assignment #1 or Assignment #2, or as a revision to follow either.

Students should find their own sources for this assignment, though they can be directed to add sources to research materials already given to them. Being required to find at least some of the research helps they learn to use the library and to justify their research selections. In any case, working on this complete AB assignment teaches students conventions of college-level research by introducing them to concepts of citation, the five types of annotation, and the format of ABs. Of course, advanced students can benefit from this assignment in the context of research projects.

Audience

Developmental composition students, first-year or advanced composition students, or students in any WAC course in which research plays a role.

Timeline

Two to five weeks. The depth of instruction needed and the number of sources students must find and annotate will affect the timeline.

Learning Outcomes / Students Will...

- Find a minimum number of appropriate sources on an approved topic of their choice.
- Produce a properly formatted AB (typically alphabetized but may be chronological or organized in any way suitable to the course).
- Produce reasonably correct bibliographic citations.
- Clearly articulate a researchable question/interest/thesis in an introductory paragraph.

- Clearly annotate a given number of sources written with combined annotations that appropriately use the other four annotation types.

Activity Description

In this assignment, students will produce an AB of whatever number of sources that you decide. The AB will include an introductory paragraph that outlines the student's topic, explains their interest in it, includes a research question, and specifies a working thesis. Students will locate their own sources. Sources may be cited in whichever style is prevalent in the course. The annotations will be written with the combined annotation form, which includes appropriate use of descriptive, summative, evaluative, and reflective annotations.

IL instruction may be unnecessary if this assignment is used as a revision exercise for a more basic preliminary AB that students have already written. For example, it can be used as a revision exercise for Assignment #1, which focuses on only descriptive and summative annotations, or Assignment #2, which allows students to write whatever kind of annotation they like. However, this assignment does pair well with IL instruction if you feel collaborative.

This assignment's focus is on producing a complete AB as a stand-alone text. It can be more motivating for students if they use their sources to write a follow-up research paper or an essay comparing the sources. Either way, students will learn how to write a combined annotation. A length requirement of 5–8 sentences will guide the students' writing. The main objectives are to get students to create an AB by crafting proper citations, writing competent combined annotations, composing a good introductory paragraph, and organizing the AB entries.

Teaching Notes

To optimize student success on this assignment, prepare lessons or work with a librarian to teach or review the basics of topic selection, resource location, citation, the format of ABs, and annotations.

This assignment's main focus is for students to learn to write an AB with the appropriate use of descriptive, summative, evaluative, and reflective elements in their combined annotations. For some sources, however, they may not need to use all four elements that constitute a robust combined annotation. In any case, you will need to prepare instructions on writing annotations (see "Chapter #3: Teaching Annotation Types").

Lower-level students, especially, need extra instructions in identifying source types for writing both citations and descriptive annotations. Students will also need to review what constitutes a good summary. Next, it makes sense to teach about writing evaluative and reflective annotations. One approach to teaching evaluative annotations is to have students consider whether an informed professional would use the source. In addition, direct them to fact-check and critique the content and to consider the author's background. To teach reflective annotations, ask students to imagine their paper and where the source might fit in their paper (e.g., as background material or as part of a main line of argument). A single lesson comparing evaluative and reflective annotations helps students differentiate between, on the one hand, assessment of a source's quality and credibility, and on the other hand, considerations about where and how the sources could be used in a paper.

Teaching this assignment with a process approach is appropriate. For example, you can ask students to do Assignment #2 (submit preliminary ABs with very brief descriptive and free-form annotations) and then, using your feedback, revise and expand their annotations for the sources they actually select. Before they write the papers, have them create a rough paper outline and try to fit the sources into it.

Other important teaching notes include the following:

- Ensure students create their AB in tandem with your instruction. After each class/lesson, require that students contribute to their AB.
- Do not underestimate how difficult it is to format an AB. Provide students a template – either in *Microsoft Word* or *Google Docs* – to guide their formatting.
- Direct students to a citation generator, handbook, library guide, or website.
- Spend sufficient time on what an AB is, what its elements are, and why you are using it as an assignment. Motivation is especially important for a first college-level research assignment.
- Instruct students on the types of annotation you require. Note that most annotations should at least briefly describe the source and include main points relevant to the research topic.

Assignments for Composition and WAC Classes   63

- Be clear about whether all or only some sources need to have a complete combined annotation utilizing all four types. For example, sources that provide only a few relevant facts may not require much summary but will still need to be described, evaluated, and reflected upon.
- Be careful: summative annotations may be overly broad or fail to capture a main line of argument. Inform students that copying an abstract, even from a database, constitutes plagiarism.
- Note that evaluative annotations are sometimes referred to as "critical annotations."

Variants

- This assignment can build on Assignments #1 or #2, or it can be a stand-alone experience.
- Students may be asked to find their sources exclusively from a particular database (e.g., *Britannica ProCon.org* or *CQ Researcher*).
- Students may be asked to find a combination of popular and scholarly sources.
- Students may be asked to write a follow-up paper comparing the sources.
- Most obviously, students may be asked to use the AB to create a research paper; they can draw from the AB to generate an outline, draft a Works Cited or References list, and select content to include in the paper.
- Students may use this assignment to prepare for a research proposal, presentation, or podcast.
- Students may use *Google Sheets* or *Microsoft Excel* for an alternative way to organize and store their work instead of creating a formal AB.
- Students may include images in their AB or even use a platform such as *Omeka* to create a digital archive.

Complete Annotated Bibliography Instructions

Overview: In this assignment, you will create a [#-source] annotated bibliography (AB) on a research topic of your choice, approved by me. Over the next [# weeks], you will incorporate feedback and revisions before submitting your complete AB. This assignment is worth [%] of your course grade. [You will/will not write a follow-up research paper. For this assignment, the AB itself is your paper.]

What is an Annotated Bibliography? A "bibliography" is an ordered list of sources – books, articles, websites, and so on – to which you refer in your work. An "annotation" is a note that is usually written to describe, summarize, evaluate, and/or reflect on a source. Thus, an "annotated bibliography" is an ordered list of citations, each one followed by an annotation.

Purpose of the Assignment: This assignment will prepare you for writing research papers.

Specific Requirements for AB:

- It will be on a topic of your choice that I must approve.
- It will contain an introductory paragraph, which will briefly discuss your research interest (why you picked the topic or what sparked your interest), tell what you hope to learn (in the form of a research question), and include a working thesis appropriate to a research paper.
- It will contain [# sources]; at least [# sources] must be found in the library's catalog or databases, and the others may be found on the Internet.
- It will follow the formatting guidelines we discuss in class and which you find modeled in the sample AB at the end of this assignment sheet.
- Each source will be cited in the [MLA] style, and the sources will be alphabetized.
- For each source, you will write a "combined" annotation. Typically, this involves describing the source, summarizing its main points and main argument, evaluating its quality, and reflecting on how it could be used in a research paper. Each annotation will be between [#–#] sentences. In class, we will discuss strategies for writing a good annotation.

Audience: You, and me as your instructor. Assume I have a working knowledge of your topic and want to learn more.
Rhetorical Purpose: To record and inform.
Assumptions: When you write your annotations, assume that you are researching the thesis from your introductory paragraph (e.g., "Youth should devote one year of service before college" or "Superman would beat Batman in battle"). You may revise your thesis before the final draft. By writing this introduction and the AB itself as if you are going to write a research paper, it will be easier to select from among the sources you find and to write your annotations.
[**Sample Annotated Bibliography:** It helps students if you include a sample AB with their assignment. See "Chapter #9: Three Sample Annotated Bibliographies" for sample ABs.]

Complete Annotated Bibliography Rubric

	Proficient	Competent	Developing	Inadequate
Introductory Paragraph	Introductory paragraph is present. Text is proficiently written, and the research question and thesis statement are well-formulated.	Introductory paragraph is present. Text is competently written, and the research question and thesis statement are fairly well-formulated.	Introductory paragraph is present. Text is indifferently written, research question is unclear or broad, or the thesis statement is broad or unclear.	Introductory paragraph is absent, unclear, or does not articulate a research question or research interest. The paragraph contains no thesis statement.
Source Quality	Found correct number and type of expert sources. Sources highly related to topic and display considerable expertise.	Found correct number and type of sources. Sources related to topic, with most displaying expertise.	Found correct number and type of sources related to topic, but some lack expertise (e.g., none from the library or its databases).	Did not find correct number or type of sources. Sources are irrelevant or only loosely related to topic.
Overall Annotation Writing Quality	Annotations conform to specified length. Annotations are well-written, grammatically sound, and fully capture the essence of sources.	Annotations conform to specified length. Annotations are well-written and adequately capture the essence of sources.	Annotations conform to specified length. Annotations are somewhat coherent and somewhat capture the essence of sources.	Annotations do not conform to specified length. Annotations are incoherent or inadequately capture the essence of sources.

	Proficient	Competent	Developing	Inadequate
Descriptive Annotation Quality	All annotations accurately describe the sources.	All annotations describe the sources, but some are inaccurate or unclear.	Most annotations describe sources, but some descriptions are missing, inaccurate, or unclear.	Few or no annotation accurately describes sources OR descriptions are missing or unclear.
Summative Annotation Quality	All summaries are accurate, include the main points and purposes of the sources, and are well paraphrased.	Most summaries are accurate, include the main points and purposes of the sources, and are well paraphrased.	Some summaries have problems with accuracy, completeness, or improper paraphrasing.	Most or all summaries are inaccurate, incomplete, or improperly paraphrased.
Evaluative Annotation Quality	All annotations thoughtfully assess the validity, reliability, and currency of the source (if relevant), and all annotations mention source quality.	Most annotations thoughtfully assess the validity, reliability, and currency of the source (if relevant). Most mention source quality.	Some annotations thoughtfully assess the validity, reliability, and currency of the source (if relevant), but some are missing or are not well-reasoned.	Few or no annotation thoughtfully assesses the validity, reliability, and currency of the source (if relevant). Source quality veritably unmentioned.
Reflective Annotation Quality	All annotations thoughtfully reflect on where and how to use the source.	Most annotations thoughtfully reflect on where and how to use the source.	Some annotations reflect on where and how to use the source, but reflections are vague.	Few or no annotation reflects on where and how to use the source.

(Continued)

	Proficient	Competent	Developing	Inadequate
Citations	Citations are entirely error-free. Formatting is correct.	Citations contain very few errors. Formatting is correct.	Citations contain some errors. Formatting is mostly correct.	Citations are absent or contain frequent errors. Formatting is incorrect.
Overall Formatting	AB is properly alphabetized, and its formatting conforms to assignment requirements with no errors.	AB is properly alphabetized, and its formatting largely conforms to assignment requirements with only 1–2 errors.	AB is not properly alphabetized, and its formatting does not conform well to assignment requirements.	AB is not properly alphabetized, and its formatting does not conform well to assignment requirements.

Any annotated bibliography that contains plagiarized material will be returned with a grade of zero (0), and appropriate steps will be taken.

Assignment #4: Annotated Bibliography and Argumentative Essay

The Annotated Bibliography and Argumentative Essay assignment addresses goals in the research and argumentative components of first-year composition, advanced composition, and some WAC courses. The main difference between this assignment and a complete AB (as in Assignment #3) is that students do their work with an eye toward forming a cogent argument to fairly represent the main perspectives on a debatable issue. Students will write a complete AB with combined annotations that appropriately use descriptive, summative, evaluative, and reflective elements. Upon completing AB, they will use their AB to plan and compose an argumentative essay.

Students find their own sources for this assignment but, as a starting point, they may be directed to a particular database appropriate to their arguments. For lower-level courses, *CQ Researcher* and *Britannica ProCon.org* are great launching pads. By conducting all or most of their own research, students develop the IL skills of finding and evaluating sources to explain the main sides of an argument. If the assignment is the students' first research writing experience, working on it will ease them into conventions of college-level research. The assignment teaches students the concepts of citation, the types of annotation, the AB, and the AB's purposeful use in writing argumentative essays.

Audience

Students in first-year composition, advanced composition, persuasive/argumentative writing, or WAC courses in which argument plays a significant role.

Timeline

Three to six weeks. The depth of instruction needed, the number of sources students must find and annotate, and the paper's length requirement will affect the timeline.

Learning Outcomes / Students Will...

- Find a minimum number of appropriate sources addressing two or more sides of a debated issue.

- Produce a properly formatted AB that is organized; this organization can be alphabetical or done by grouping pro/con/neutral sources.
- Produce reasonably correct bibliographic citations.
- Write a clear introductory paragraph articulating their topic, interest, researchable question, and debatable thesis.
- Clearly annotate a given number of sources written with combined annotations that address each source's main and supporting arguments.
- Learn to use ABs to plan and draft a researched argument.

Activity Description

This assignment fits in argumentative writing units. Students will produce an AB of however many sources you deem fit. The AB will include an introductory paragraph that outlines the topic and their research interest, poses a research question, and specifies a debatable thesis. Students will locate their own sources and cite them in whichever style you choose. They will write combined annotations that include appropriate use of descriptive, summative, evaluative, and reflective elements of say, 5–8 sentences per combined annotation.

This assignment's main objective is to help students create and use an AB as an integral part of planning and drafting an argumentative essay. The research question and working thesis in the AB's introductory paragraph will help students locate relevant sources. The assignment works best if students write a preliminary AB first (see Assignment #2), and then revise their short annotations by expanding them. This process helps students learn more about high-quality research, citations, annotations, proper organization, and the use of the AB in research and composing.

IL instruction, if used, can include a lesson on finding good sources to support and counter the students' own position. This is important because finding counterarguments can be a stumbling block for students who are used to finding echo-chamber research.

Teaching Notes

Whether this is students' first AB or the first AB written for an argumentative essay, some instruction is necessary. The need for instruction on citing sources will depend on students' experience.

However, because this assignment emphasizes argument, lessons on locating and citing sources might well be accompanied by lessons on evaluating sources (not only for general quality, but also for positionality). For example, perhaps students should be encouraged to find an equal number of peer-reviewed sources on either side of a debate. They may find that one side or another is notably absent in peer-reviewed literature.

By embedding this assignment in an argumentative writing unit, you will help students to practice researching a debatable issue and composing a balanced argumentative essay. In requiring sources that flesh out a debate, you will help students avoid cut-and-paste use of passages and the use of only sources that support their position. Consider a lesson on organizing the AB in a way that highlights distinct arguments and counterarguments, and to use the AB to plan and draft argumentative essays.

Unless students have previously completed an AB, you will need to prepare instruction on the five annotation types (see "Chapter #3: Teaching Annotation Types"). Using a process approach, students can submit preliminary ABs with brief descriptive and summative annotations. With feedback on a preliminary AB, they can decide which sources seem most appropriate to use in their papers. Having received feedback, students will likely need instruction on creating evaluative and reflective annotations. Teaching these forms together helps students differentiate between evaluating source quality/credibility and reflecting on where/how to use arguments and counterarguments in their papers. They can then complete their existing annotations and add in additional sources to fill research gaps.

To ensure that writing the AB is not merely busywork, it is important to promise students that the assignment can teach them to use ABs efficiently. Even before they have turned in their completed ABs, you can make good on this promise. One class period can be devoted to organizing ABs into arguments and counterarguments. Another class period can be spent turning an AB into a rough outline by pasting annotative content wherever it fits (but remind students to keep track of who says what if they parcel out a single annotation into different sections of their outline). Another class can be devoted to modeling how to turn the outline into a rough draft, omitting the unnecessary parts of the annotation. You will need to model these processes because they are not always obvious.

Other important teaching notes:
- Ensure students create their AB in tandem with your instruction by contributing something to their AB after each lesson, be it a source of support, opposition, or neutral background.
- Provide students a template in *Microsoft Word* or *Google Docs* to help them format their ABs.
- Let students know how writing ABs can help them develop fair and balanced arguments.
- Instruct students on the annotation types. Most annotations should, at minimum, briefly describe the source, as well as evaluate its arguments.
- Be clear about your requirements for combined annotations, especially whether students need to use all elements of combined annotation for every source. For example, sources that provide only a few relevant facts may not require much summary but will need to be described, evaluated, and reflected upon.
- Even upper-level students may need reminders about what makes a useful summary. Summative annotations may be too broad or fail to capture the main line of argument.
- One hopes your students will not need a lesson on why copying abstracts constitutes plagiarism.
- Note that evaluative annotations are sometimes referred to as "critical annotations."

Variants

- Students may be asked to find their sources exclusively from a particular database (e.g., *Britannica ProCon.org* or *CQ Researcher*).
- Students may be asked to find a combination of popular and scholarly sources.
- Students may use this unit to prepare for a class debate or a presentation/podcast.

Annotated Bibliography and Argumentative Essay Instructions

Overview: In this assignment, you will create an [#-source] annotated bibliography (AB) on a researchable, debatable topic that meets my approval. Over the next [# weeks], you will incorporate feedback and revisions before submitting your completed AB. This assignment is worth [%] of your course grade. You will then use the AB to plan and write an argumentative essay. [Attach your argumentative essay instructions.]

What is an Annotated Bibliography? A "bibliography" is an ordered list of sources – books, articles, websites, and so on – to which you refer in your work. An "annotation" is a note that is usually written to describe, summarize, evaluate, and/or reflect on a source. Thus, an "annotated bibliography" is an ordered list of citations, each one followed by an annotation.

Purpose of the Assignment: In this assignment, you will learn to create an AB and to use it to plan and write a researched argumentative paper.

Specific Requirements for AB:

- It will be on a debatable and researchable topic of your choice that I must approve.
- It will contain an introductory paragraph, which will briefly discuss why you picked the topic (what sparked your interest), tell what you hope to learn (research question), and include your position on the topic (debatable thesis).
- It will contain [# sources]; you will find at least [# sources] in the library's catalog or databases.
- It will follow the formatting guidelines we discuss in class and which you find modeled in the sample AB at the end of this assignment sheet.
- Each source will be cited in the [MLA] style, and sources will be organized by pro/con/neutrality.
- For each source, you will write a "combined" annotation. Typically, this involves describing the source, summarizing its main points and main argument, evaluating its quality, and reflecting on how it could be used in a

research paper. Each annotation will be between [#–#] sentences. In class, we will discuss strategies for writing a good annotation.

Audience: You, me as your instructor, and an audience interested in this debate. Assume your audience has a working knowledge of your topic and wants to learn more.

Rhetorical Purpose: To record and inform.

Assumptions: When writing annotations, research the question and thesis statement from your introductory paragraph (e.g., "Youth should devote a year of service before college" or "The use of artificial intelligence promotes invasion of privacy"). You can revise the thesis as you proceed.

You will use your completed AB to create an outline and draft your argumentative essay.

[**Sample Annotated Bibliography:** It helps students if you include a sample AB with their assignment. See "Chapter #9: Three Sample Annotated Bibliographies" for sample ABs.]

Annotated Bibliography and Argumentative Essay Rubric

	Proficient	Competent	Developing	Inadequate
Introduction	Introductory paragraph is proficiently written, and the research question and debatable thesis are well-formulated.	Introductory paragraph is competently written, and the research question and debatable thesis are fairly well-formulated.	Introductory paragraph is indifferently written. The research question or debatable thesis is unclear or broad.	Introductory paragraph is absent, unclear, or does not articulate the research question or debatable thesis.
Source Quality	Found correct number and type of sources. Sources highly related to topic and display considerable expertise.	Found correct number and type of sources. Sources related to topic, with most displaying expertise.	Found correct number and type of sources. Sources related to topic, though may lack a degree of expertise (e.g., none from library or databases).	Did not find correct number or type of sources. Sources are irrelevant or only loosely related to topic.
Annotation Writing Quality	Annotations conform to specified length, are well-written, grammatically sound, and fully capture the essence of sources.	Annotations conform to specified length, are reasonably well-written, and adequately capture the essence of sources.	Annotations conform to specified length but are occasionally unclear or too brief, failing to capture the essence of some sources.	Annotations do not conform to specified length and are incoherent or inadequately capture the essence of sources.

(Continued)

	Proficient	Competent	Developing	Inadequate
Use of Annotation Elements in Combined Annotations	All annotations appropriately describe the sources, summarize the relevant parts of the argument, evaluate the source quality, and reflect on the source's utility, given your argument.	Most, but not all, annotations appropriately describe the sources, summarize the relevant parts of the argument, evaluate the source quality, and reflect on the source's utility, given your argument.	Some annotations appropriately describe the sources, summarize the relevant parts of the argument, evaluate the source quality, and reflect on the source's utility, given your argument.	Few or no annotation appropriately describes the sources, summarize the relevant parts of the argument, evaluate the source quality, and reflect on the source's utility, given your argument.
Citation Format	Citations are entirely error-free. Formatting is correct.	Citations contain very few errors. Formatting is correct.	Citations contain some errors. Formatting is mostly correct.	Citations are absent or contain frequent errors. Formatting is incorrect.
Overall Formatting	AB conforms to assignment organization and formatting requirements with no errors.	AB largely conforms to assignment organization and formatting requirements with few errors.	AB does not conform well to assignment formatting or its organization requirements.	AB is not well organized, and its formatting does not conform well to assignment requirements.

Any annotated bibliography that contains plagiarized material will be returned with a grade of zero (0), and appropriate steps will be taken.

Assignment #5: Bibliographic Essay

The Bibliographic Essay assignment is appropriate for upper-level composition and graduate courses. The assignment builds on research skills acquired in first-year composition courses. Students will write a complete AB using combined annotations with descriptive, summative, evaluative, and/or reflective components. However, instead of writing a traditional AB and research paper, they will organize the AB by subtopic and then use it to write a bibliographic essay for a research audience. The assignment's purpose is to help students understand how to gain control over a body of research in a way that prepares them well for advanced research writing.

Students find their own sources for this assignment, building expertise in advanced research. They may begin with a broader topic than might be typical of a short research paper or with a topic that they attempt to research exhaustively (e.g., a senior seminar paper). The bibliographic essay is likely to be a new genre for students, and they will learn to reflect on the utility of research for a particular audience. Ideally, their AB and bibliographic essay is followed by a research proposal and/or paper in which they use relevant parts of their work.

Audience

Students in advanced composition courses, upper-level WAC courses, and graduate courses in any field.

Timeline

Eight to sixteen weeks. The depth of instruction needed, the number of sources students must find and annotate, and the paper's length requirement will affect the timeline.

Learning Outcomes / Students Will...

- Find a minimum number of appropriate sources.
- Produce a properly formatted AB organized by subtopic [and possibly alphabetized or chronologized within subtopics].
- Produce correct bibliographic citations.
- Write a clear introduction in the AB that sets out a research question, scope, appropriate audience(s), and the student's research path.

- Clearly annotate sources with combined annotations that appropriately use the other four annotation types.
- Learn to adapt an AB into a bibliographic essay.
- Become familiar with a body of research.

Activity Description

This assignment fits well within the scope of an upper-level, senior seminar, or graduate course. Students will produce an AB of whatever number of sources you deem fit. The AB will include an introduction that clearly explains the research question, scope of the AB, appropriate audience(s), and student's research path. This will almost certainly need to be revised as they proceed. Students will locate their own sources and cite them in whichever style is preferred in the course. They will write combined annotations that appropriately use descriptive, summative, evaluative, and reflective elements – all written with their research question and audience in mind. They will then use the AB to plan and draft a bibliographic essay.

The AB may be constructed without IL instruction, especially if students have been thoroughly introduced to library resources and specialized databases. However, it may be helpful to include one or more IL sessions on finding appropriate sources. Students should be encouraged to find more sources than they think they will need, and they can, of course, pare down their sources as they proceed.

This assignment's main objective is for students to write an AB that will help them draft a bibliographic essay. As a major research assignment, this experience introduces students to a new form of advanced scholarship. The AB's introduction, even in draft form, helps students locate relevant sources while keeping their audience in mind. In short, students will improve at their research writing!

Teaching Notes

To optimize student success on this assignment, prepare instruction that addresses audience identification (given their topic), source location, types of annotation, and the format and purpose of ABs and bibliographic essays. Plan to model the use of ABs in creating plans/outlines and drafts of their bibliographic essays. It is likely students will have had some experience citing sources, although potentially not in the particular documentation style associated with the course, so you may need to provide appropriate citation resources.

This assignment assumes students have research writing experience, but that they may be unfamiliar with ABs. Decide on the extent of instruction they need regarding annotation types. Students will probably know how to summarize, but will need direction on writing summative annotations that focus on the needs of a research audience. Similarly, students will need some guidance in evaluating and reflecting on sources for their particular audience. If the class takes a process approach, students could submit a preliminary AB and then revise it with instructor and peer feedback. See "Chapter #3: Teaching Annotation Types" for more information.

You will need to discuss the organization of the AB. Alphabetized ABs may be preferable, but they can also be organized by subtopic, audience, or chronology to facilitate writing a bibliographic essay. If organization by subtopic is used, specify whether students can or should use the same sources in different sections (possibly with different annotations).

Instruction should be devoted to writing an introduction for both the AB and the bibliographic essay. At minimum, both introductions should specify the research question, explain the scope of the research, suggest appropriate audience(s), and outline the student's research path (e.g., "The ProQuest One Business database was used; one hundred potential sources were identified, and twenty sources were selected for inclusion"). It helps to have a model bibliographic essay that you deem appropriate. See "Chapter #9: Sample Annotated Bibliographies" for model ABs.

Because the bibliographic essay is a new form, you may need to model how to take passages from the AB and transform them for the bibliographic essay. This would include modeling the process of cutting irrelevant components from annotations and adding sentences that turn the AB into a coherent bibliographic essay.

Other important teaching notes include the following:

- Ensure students create their AB in tandem with your instruction, allowing sufficient time for revision and for writing the bibliographic essay.
- Students will have difficulties formatting their ABs and writing bibliographic essays. Consider providing them templates.
- Spend sufficient time comparing the AB to a bibliographic essay, including the elements that go into each, how to organize the sources in each, and the purpose of these two genres.

- Show students how to adapt their annotations to their purpose and audience.
- Be clear about whether all, or only some, sources need to have a complete combined annotation. For example, annotations of sources that provide only a few relevant facts may not require much summary, but will still need to be descriptive, evaluative, and reflective.
- Students may have difficulty handling organization if a source fits in more than one area of their AB and bibliographic essay. Advise them to be succinct if they mention a source a second time.

Variants

- Students may be asked to find their sources exclusively from a particular database.
- Students may be asked to present their work or create a podcast from it.
- Students may be asked to write a follow-up research proposal and/or research paper.
- Students who have excelled may be encouraged to submit their essays for publication.
- With broad topics, students may work on collaborative ABs and write individual bibliographic essays.
- The AB and bibliographic essay may be written for a professional audience, such as active teachers, in which case students may find popular, professional, or scholarly sources. Consider the case of teachers assembling reading lists, organized by Lexile levels, of popular children's works and then writing an accompanying bibliographic essay explaining the project.

Annotated Bibliography with Bibliographic Essay Instructions

Overview: In this assignment, you will create an [#-source] annotated bibliography (AB) on a research topic of your choice, approved by me, and then convert the AB into a bibliographic essay. Over the next [# weeks], you will incorporate feedback before submitting your completed AB and bibliographic essay. This AB is worth [%] and the bibliographic essay is worth [%] of the course grade.

What is an Annotated Bibliography? Recall that an "annotated bibliography" (AB) is an ordered list of citations, each one followed by an annotation about the source.

Purpose of the Assignment: This assignment will introduce you to the bibliography essay, a publishable genre that can initiate a research project. Your goal is to find and organize research [by subtopic] as you consider the sources' contribution to the field, and to use the AB to generate a bibliographic essay also organized [by subtopic] and appropriate for a particular audience.

Specific Requirements for AB:

- It will be on a topic of your choice that I must approve.
- It will contain an introduction that sets out the research question, scope of the AB, appropriate audience(s), and research path that you use to find sources.
- It will contain [#] reputable sources [mostly found in the library's catalog or databases].
- It will follow the formatting guidelines we discuss in class and which you find modeled in the sample AB at the end of this assignment sheet.
- Each source will be cited in the [MLA/APA/Chicago] format.
- Sources will be grouped by subtopic [and arranged alphabetically or chronologically within each subtopic]. A source may appear in two subtopic areas but count as one source.
- For each source, you will write a "combined" annotation, typically between [#-#] sentences, that appropriately describes, summarizes, evaluates, and reflects on

whether and how you will use the source in your research [or professionals or scholars could use the source in their research.]

Specific Requirements for Bibliographic Essay

- It will contain an introduction revised from the AB introduction.
- It will contain [#] reputable sources [mostly found in the library's catalog or databases].
- It will be organized appropriately; each section will explain how various sources are relevant for further research in the topic, drawing from the annotations in your AB.
- The paragraphs will be written in standard essay style and form.
- The conclusion will suggest avenues of further work/research on the topic.
- It will follow [APA/MLA/Chicago] formatting guidelines.

Audience: You, me as your instructor, and other interested professionals.
Rhetorical Purpose: To inform in an organized way.
[**Samples:** It helps students if you include a sample AB and bibliographic essay with their assignment. See "Chapter #9: Three Sample Annotated Bibliographies" for sample ABs.]

Annotated Bibliography with Bibliographic Essay Rubric

	Proficient	Competent	Developing	Inadequate
Introductory Paragraph (AB and Essay)	Introduction is proficiently written, clearly explaining the topic, question, scope of the research, and research path.	Introduction is competently written, but there are some gaps as it explains the topic, question, scope of the research, and research path.	Introduction is indifferently written. It is unclear or unfocused in explaining the topic, question, scope of the research, and the research path.	Introduction is absent, unclear, or shallow as it explains the topic, question, scope of the research, or research path.
Source Quality (AB and Essay)	Found correct number of expert sources that are highly relevant to topic.	Found correct number of sources relevant to topic, with most displaying expertise.	Found correct number of sources relevant to topic, though some may lack a degree of expertise.	Did not find correct number of sources, or many sources are irrelevant or of low quality.
Overall Annotation Writing Quality (AB only)	Combined annotations are well-written and fully capture the essence and importance of sources.	Combined annotations are well-written and adequately capture the essence and importance of sources.	Combined annotations are largely coherent and somewhat capture the essence and importance of sources.	Many combined annotations are vague or inadequately capture the essence and importance of sources.

(Continued)

	Proficient	Competent	Developing	Inadequate
Organization and Coherence (Bibliographic Essay)	Bibliographic essay is cogently written, follows organization guidelines, and does an excellent job explaining how sources contribute to research/work on the topic.	Bibliographic essay is mostly well-written, follows organization guidelines, and does a good job explaining how most sources contribute to research/work on the topic.	Bibliographic essay is indifferently written, has organizational problems, or shallowly explains how sources contribute to research/work on the topic.	Bibliographic essay is poorly written, disorganized, fails to use the guidelines, and/or shallowly explains how sources contribute to research/work on the topic.
Conclusion (Bibliographic Essay)	Conclusion is well-written, suggesting interesting and clear possibilities for future work.	Conclusion is clearly written, suggesting some possibilities for future work.	Conclusion is somewhat shallow, broad, or unclear as it suggests possibilities for future work.	Conclusion is poorly written or has very few, very vague, or very unclear possibilities for future work.
Citations (AB and Essay)	Citations are entirely error-free. Formatting is correct.	Citations contain very few errors. Formatting is correct.	Citations contain some errors. Formatting is mostly correct.	Citations are absent or contain frequent errors. Formatting is incorrect.
Formatting (AB and Essay)	AB and essay meet format requirements with no errors.	AB and essay meet format requirements with only 1–2 errors.	AB and essay meet format requirements with a few errors.	AB and essay do not meet format requirements or are largely incorrect.

Any annotated bibliography or bibliographic essay that contains plagiarized material will be returned with a grade of zero (0), and appropriate steps will be taken.

Assignment #6: Collaborative Annotated Bibliography

The Collaborative Annotated Bibliography assignment addresses goals in the research component of composition or WAC courses. Students will work in groups or as a whole class to write a complete AB with combined annotations that incorporate descriptive, summative, evaluative, and reflective elements. They will then use selections from the collaborative AB to plan and draft a research paper, either individually or in a group. This assignment works well in theme-based courses or units in which students read and write about a common topic.

Students find their own sources in cooperation with their group members. By conducting their own research, students learn to use the library and to justify source selections. Working collaboratively allows students to learn from one another about college-level research as they compose citations and annotations. Using the AB purposefully to plan and compose their research papers introduces students to concepts of professional research.

Audience

Students in any composition or WAC course with a research-writing component.

Timeline

Five to ten weeks, depending on the depth of instruction and the number of sources required.

Learning Outcomes / Students Will...

- Find a minimum number of appropriate sources.
- Contribute to an AB formatted and organized appropriately (e.g., alphabetically, chronologically, or by subtopic).
- Produce reasonably correct bibliographic citations.
- Annotate a given number of sources with well-written combined annotations that appropriately use descriptive, summative, evaluative, and reflective annotative elements.
- Learn to use ABs to collaboratively plan and draft a research paper.
- Practice collaborative writing.

Activity Description

This assignment fits into most courses requiring research. Students will contribute to a collaboratively written AB with whatever number of sources you deem fit. They will cite sources in whichever style is prevalent in the course. Students will create combined annotations with appropriate descriptive, summative, evaluative, and/or reflective elements. The AB has an introductory paragraph that outlines the topic, poses one or more research questions, and – depending on whether there is an individual or group paper – includes one or more thesis statements. Each group member will locate sources to add to a shared AB. One they have created a shared AB, groups can write a collaborative paper on a shared thesis or, alternatively, students can write individual papers. Students will pare down their sources as they proceed.

The AB may be constructed without IL instruction, especially if the class includes lessons on finding appropriate sources or if students are directed to selected databases. However, this assignment's main objective is to help students improve their research-writing skills through collaboration and through the construction of ABs as an organic part of the research process. The assignment will teach them how to cite sources correctly, and how to write good combined annotations that describe, summarize, evaluate, and/or reflect upon each source.

Teaching Notes

To optimize success on this assignment, prepare lessons or work with a librarian to teach students about topic selection, resource location, citation, AB formatting, the types of annotation, and the use of ABs to plan and draft a research paper. If this is the students' first major research assignment, they will be unfamiliar with ABs and how to conduct college-level research. Ultimately, the goal is for students to practice scholarly research writing that moves past a mere cut-and-paste use of sources. They will learn to write an AB with combinations of descriptive, summative, evaluative, and reflective elements. A length requirement per annotation will guide them. They will also learn to use the AB to plan and draft their research papers. Unless they have already written a complete AB in an earlier course, you will need to prepare instruction on the five types of annotation. See "Chapter #3: Teaching Annotation Types" for more information.

If you use a process approach, students can submit preliminary ABs with brief descriptive and summative annotations after a review of how these two types of annotation should be written. With feedback on their preliminary ABs, students can decide which sources seem most appropriate for their papers. Having received feedback, students will likely need instruction on creating evaluative and reflective annotations. Teaching these forms together helps students differentiate between, on the one hand, evaluating source quality/credibility and, on the other hand, reflecting on where/how to use sources in their papers. After this instruction, they can then complete their existing annotations and add in additional sources to fill research gaps.

The collaborative approach, whether small-group or whole-class, provides an avenue to foster high-quality and relevant research, proper citations, and well-written annotations. Developing and advanced students alike will, undoubtedly, learn from one another as they compare their work, especially if all students are required to write an annotation on a common text. Furthermore, students will see differences in the quality of the sources and learn that sources can be used for multiple purposes. They may even find themselves fact-checking one another if different sources provide "alternative facts" about the topic.

Because students are working collaboratively, instruction on how to cite sources should include a peer-review experience so students can help one another learn about citation and can proof one another's work. The use of a collaboration tool, such as a shared *Google Sheet*, can ease this process, with students entering citation information in one column and annotations in another. Peer review can be conducted using the same tool. Whether students ultimately produce a collaborative research paper or use a shared AB to produce their own individual paper is up to you.

To ensure that students see the AB assignment as more than busywork, teach them to use their ABs efficiently to make their research writing more efficient and effective. For example, a class period can focus on how to select material from annotations and paste it into an outline (but warn students to cite authors if they use one source/annotation in *multiple* sections of an outline). As a follow-up, you can devote a class period to turning their outlines into rough drafts, omitting any unnecessary material. You will need to model these processes because they are not always obvious.

Other important teaching notes include the following:

- Ensure students create their AB in tandem with your instruction. After each class/lesson, require them to contribute something to their AB, be it an introductory paragraph, potential resources, a citation, or a preliminary annotation. Keep them working!
- Provide students a template – either in *Word* or *Google Docs* format – to guide their formatting.
- Spend sufficient time on what an AB is, the elements it has, and its purpose in research-writing.
- Instruct students on the annotation types. Note: most annotations should, at minimum, briefly describe and include relevant points from the source.
- Be clear about whether or not all sources need to have a complete combined annotation. For example, annotations of sources that provide only a few relevant facts may not require much summary, but will need descriptive, evaluative, and reflective elements.
- Students' summative annotations may be too broad or fail to capture a main line of argument.
- You may need a lesson on why copying abstracts constitutes plagiarism.
- Note that evaluative annotations are often referred to as "critical" annotations.

Variants

- The whole class can have one topic or a group can have different topics.
- The assignment fits well in topic-driven courses, such as writing-about-writing composition classes.
- Instead of writing a traditional AB, students can use shared *Excel* or *Google Sheets* to record their citations and annotations (and to conduct peer review).
- Individual students or groups can write a follow-up research paper.
- Students may engage in a debate if pro/con teams are set up.
- Students may use the AB to create a research proposal and/or presentation.
- Students may use *Excel* or *Google Sheets* in lieu of creating a formal AB.

Collaborative Annotated Bibliography Instructions

Overview: In this assignment, you will create an [#-source] annotated bibliography (AB) with your group on a topic of your group's choice, approved by me. Each group member will contribute [#] annotations to the AB. Over the next [# weeks], you will incorporate feedback and revisions before submitting your completed AB. This assignment is worth [%] of your course grade. You [will/will not] use the AB to plan and write a research paper. [Attach research paper instructions.]

What is an Annotated Bibliography? A "bibliography" is an ordered list of sources – books, articles, websites, and so on – to which you refer in your work. An "annotation" is a note written to describe, summarize, evaluate, and/or reflect on a source, and a combined annotation includes two or more of the other annotation types. Thus, an "annotated bibliography" is an ordered list of citations, each one followed by an annotation.

Purpose of the Assignment: This assignment will help you learn more about conducting high-quality research and how to do collaborative writing.

Specific Requirements for AB:

- It will be on a topic that your group chooses and that I must approve.
- It will contain an introductory paragraph, which will briefly discuss why your group picked the topic (e.g., what sparked your interest), tell what you hope to learn (in the form of a research question), and include a working thesis.
- It will contain [# total sources], of which [#] must be contributed by each group member. Each group member will find at least [#] sources in the library's catalog or databases.
- It will follow the formatting guidelines we discuss in class and which you find modeled in the sample AB at the end of this assignment sheet.
- Each source will be cited in the [MLA] style, and sources will be ordered [alphabetically].

> - Each source will have a combined annotation that draws from the other four types of annotation: descriptive, summative, evaluative, and reflective. Most annotations will be between [#–#] sentences. We will discuss strategies for writing a good annotation in class.
>
> **Audience:** Your group, and me as your instructor. Assume I have a working knowledge of your topic and want to learn more.
>
> **Rhetorical Purpose:** To record and inform.
>
> **Assumptions:** When writing annotations, focus on your research question(s) and thesis statement from your introductory paragraph. You can revise these along the way.
>
> [Take your research seriously: your group will use your completed AB to create an outline and rough draft of your research paper.]
>
> [**Sample Annotated Bibliography:** It helps students if you include a sample AB with their assignment. See "Chapter #9: Three Sample Annotated Bibliographies" for sample ABs.]

Collaborative Annotated Bibliography Rubric

For the Collaborative Annotated Bibliography assignment, use the rubric from Assignment #3: Complete Annotated Bibliography.

Works Cited

Nielsen, Danielle. "Universal Design in First-Year Composition – Why Do We Need It, How Can We Do It?" *The CEA Forum*, vol. 42, no. 2, 2013, https://is.gd/AoREdL.

Further Reading

Association of College and Research Libraries. *Framework for Information Literacy for Higher Education*. American Library Association, 2016, https://is.gd/RSmGkY.
Aull, Laura. "Corpus Analysis of Argumentative Versus Explanatory Discourse in Writing Task Genres." *The Journal of Writing Analytics*, vol. 1, no. 1, 2017, pp. 1–47, https://doi.org/10.37514/JWA-J.2017.1.1.03.
Beatty, Luke, and Cynthia A. Cochran. *Writing the Annotated Bibliography: A Guide for Students and Researchers*. Routledge, 2020, https://doi.org/10.4324/9780367853051.

Berry, Bridget, et al. "'It's a Practice Thing': The Annotated Bibliography as a Learning Activity for Arts Students." *Synergy*, no. 31, 2011, pp. 24–31, https://is.gd/nx8Hku.

Birkett, Melissa, and Amy Hughes. "A Collaborative Project to Integrate Information Literacy Skills into an Undergraduate Psychology Course." *Psychology Learning & Teaching*, vol. 12, no. 1, 2013, pp. 96–100, https://doi.org/10.2304/plat.2013.12.1.96.

Edwards, Mary E., and Erik W. Black. "Contemporary Instructor-Librarian Collaboration: A Case Study of an Online Embedded Librarian Implementation." *Journal of Library & Information Services in Distance Learning*, vol. 6, no. 3–4, 2012, pp. 284–311, https://doi.org/10.1080/1533290X.2012.705690.

Fitzpatrick, Damian, and Tracey Costley. "Using Annotated Bibliographies to Develop Student Writing in Social Sciences." *Discipline-Specific Writing: Theory into Practice*, edited by John Flowerdew and Tracey Costley, Routledge, 2017, pp. 113–25, https://doi.org/10.4324/9781315519012.

Hosier, Allison. "Teaching Information Literacy through 'Un-Research.'" *Communications in Information Literacy*, vol. 9, no. 2, 2015, pp. 126–35, https://doi.org/10.15760/comminfolit.2015.9.2.189.

Insua, Glenda M., et al. "In Their Own Words: Using First-Year Student Research Journals to Guide Information Literacy Instruction." *Portal: Libraries and the Academy*, vol. 18, no. 1, 2018, pp. 141–61, https://doi.org/10.1353/pla.2018.0007.

Jones, Leigh A. "Podcasting and Performativity: Multimodal Invention in an Advanced Writing Class." *Composition Studies*, vol. 38, no. 2, 2010, pp. 75–91, https://is.gd/bHN2aA.

Koss, Lorelei. "Writing and Information Literacy in a Cryptology First-Year Seminar." *Cryptologia*, vol. 38, no. 3, 2014, pp. 223–31, https://doi.org/10.1080/01611194.2014.915256.

Lidzy, Sheryl. "'Doing Business In...': An Emic Training Module." *Journal of the Communication, Speech & Theatre Association of North Dakota*, vol. 23, 2011/2010, pp. 49–55.

Mackey, Thomas P., and Trudi Jacobson. "Integrating Information Literacy in Lower- and Upper-Level Courses: Developing Scalable Models for Higher Education." *The Journal of General Education*, vol. 53, no. 3, 2004, pp. 201–24, https://doi.org/10.1353/jge.2005.0006.

Parkes, Mitchell, et al. "Collaborative Annotated Bibliographies: An Online Strategy to Foster Student Collaboration and Understanding." *Proceedings of EdMedia 2013--World Conference on Educational Media and Technology*, Association for the Advancement of Computing in Education (AACE), 2013, pp. 2205–11, https://is.gd/x7QUzh.

Rinto, Erin E. "Developing and Applying an Information Literacy Rubric to Student Annotated Bibliographies." *Evidence Based Library and Information Practice*, vol. 8, no. 3, 2013, pp. 5–18, https://doi.org/10.18438/B8559F.

Risanti, Yanidya Ulfa. "The Undergraduate Students Critical Thinking in Writing Evaluative Annotated Bibliography in Extensive Reading Class." *RETAIN: Research on English Language Teaching in Indonesia*, vol. 7, no. 1, 2019, pp. 80–89, https://is.gd/hRkUon.

Roberson, Julie, and Jenny Horton. "Creating a Combination IL and English Composition Course in a College Setting." *Best Practices for Credit-Bearing Information Literacy Courses*, edited by Christopher Vance Hollister, Association of College and Research Libraries, 2010, pp. 65–76, https://is.gd/wrHM6F.

Russom, Caroline L. "First Year Research and Writing Convergences." *Academic Exchange Quarterly*, vol. 7, no. 3, 2003, pp. 194–98.

Sample, Mark. "Sharing Research and Building Knowledge through Zotero." *Learning Through Digital Media: Experiments in Technology and Pedagogy*, edited by R. Trebor Scholz, Institute for Distributed Creativity, 2011, pp. 295–303, https://is.gd/Hf43eE.

Stadler, Derek. *Writing Effective Annotated Bibliographies Using Blackboard's Discussion Board*. CUNY LaGuardia Community College, 2018, https://is.gd/Ylry7P.

Tan-de Ramos, Jennifer. "Effects of Teaching Strategies in Annotated Bibliography Writing." *Journal of Education and Practice*, vol. 6, no. 7, 2015, pp. 54–57, https://is.gd/uFU4KD.

Walsh, Lynda, et al. "The Burkean Parlor as Boundary Object: A Collaboration between First-Year Writing and the Library." *Composition Studies*, vol. 46, no. 1, 2018, pp. 103–23, https://is.gd/NEXHZH.

5 Librarian Assignments

Luke Beatty

Introduction

This chapter contains seven annotated bibliography (AB) assignments I designed for librarians teaching credit-bearing information literacy (IL) courses at the undergraduate level. To avoid unnecessary repetition, I have prepended a series of Common Elements sections before the assignments. These sections contain preparatory activities, background work, design principles, and an assignment sheet that apply to all of the subsequent assignments. In the interest of getting the most out of the chapter, I recommend reading the Common Elements sections first and then working through the assignments that pique your interest. Feel free to use any of the assignment sheets, rubrics, and standards alignments in this chapter for educational, non-commercial use.

In addition to the Common Elements sections, each assignment in this chapter includes the following elements:

- Outcome(s) – What students are expected to learn from the assignment.
- Standards – Relevant professional standards for the assignment.
- Baseline Assignment Sheet Changes – Any deviations from the Common Elements assignment sheet.
- Teaching Notes – Things to keep in mind when rolling out the assignment.
- Rubric – A tailored rubric for the assignment.
- Further Reading – Literature touching on similar or related assignments. Those wanting to see how others have handled "my" assignments will find these sources quite helpful.
- With that as background, read on.

Common Elements – Information Literacy Instruction

I designed the assignments in this chapter for credit-bearing IL courses taught by librarians. Such courses are now common in higher education and are often taught within general education programs or alongside first-year writing classes. Credit-bearing IL courses typically instruct students about how to find, document, and evaluate information, and because AB assignments also get at these skills, the AB is a natural fit in IL courses.

When deployed alongside your IL instruction, AB assignments should ease students into the conventions of research, citation, and annotation. Consequently, you will need to prepare a suite of IL lessons covering topic selection, material location, citation, source evaluation, and annotation writing. I leave the specifics of these lessons to you, but for the AB assignments in this chapter to succeed, your students must have a modest IL foundation in place. Librarians wanting a refresher on ABs should consult "Chapter #3: Teaching Annotation Types." Those looking to support ABs outside the classroom should see "Chapter #6: Library Support."

In designing your IL lessons, work under the assumption that the majority of your students will be unfamiliar with how to conduct college-level research. As such, I would scaffold your AB assignment in tandem with your IL lessons. For example, in one week, students will handle part x of the AB; in the next week, they will handle part y; and so on. Check in with students periodically to ensure they are on track. In addition, recognize that writing annotations will be mystifying for many students, and so be prepared to instruct them on how to write a "proper" annotation. Regardless of where your IL instruction takes you, remember to emphasize that student work must be clear and thoroughly edited.

Common Elements – Citation

To successfully write ABs, students must first understand how to cite sources. With that said, I am *not* a believer that bibliographic instruction should feature heavily in your IL program. After all, is being able to produce an error-free list of references really a valuable learning objective? ("No," in my opinion.) My advice, then, is to quickly and practically get students ready for producing citations as follows:

- Devote a little time to explaining why formal citations are expected in higher education.

- Model how to use plug-and-play citation generators (see https://library.ic.edu/cite for examples).
- Note the formatting conventions – in particular, indentation – associated with most citation styles.
- Remind students that the rules governing citations can be found in style manuals, handbooks, or guides available through your library.

I recommend designing some activities that speak to the above and calling it a day. One caveat, however: certain members of the professoriate still maintain hardline attitudes about the value of perfect citations, and those attitudes can (and will!) frustrate students who have better things to do. Advise students to discover whether their professors will be lenient or severe with citations; if the latter, suggest that after generating citations online, students should clean them up with manuals, handbooks, or library guides. Or, better yet, have them come see you if they expect citational trouble.

Common Elements – Formatting

Do not trivialize the difficulty students have in formatting their ABs. It is tricky, after all: different indents, esoteric layouts, hard and soft returns, and so on. To help them along, I provide students with a sample AB – downloadable in either *Word* or *Google Docs* format – so they can simplify their formatting and focus on the stuff that really matters. As with producing note-perfect citations, I question whether formatting an AB is truly a worthwhile learning objective. (Again, I suspect "no.") If students have the wherewithal to use your template properly, grade them as if they had formatted the AB themselves.

Common Elements – Assignment Design

If you adapt any of the AB assignments in this chapter, I recommend keeping two points in mind:

- Assignment transparency is paramount.
- Scaffolding assignments alongside your IL instruction is a winning strategy.

Regarding assignment transparency, be explicit about what your assignment involves, how students can succeed, and when the assignment is due. Ensure your assignment includes detailed requirements, a rubric, and an explanation of what students will learn by doing it. With regard to assignment sequencing, there is considerable scholarship about how scaffolded instruction helps students learn. With that in mind, I recommend your IL lessons and check-in schedules correspond with assignment benchmarks. For example, after you have taught a lesson on, say, finding books in the library catalog, ensure that students find a couple of books for their ABs before next class.

Common Elements – Assignment Sheet

Below, you will find a sample assignment sheet that pairs with Assignment #1: The Simplest Annotated Bibliography and serves as the baseline assignment sheet for all other assignments in this chapter. So as not to reproduce this sheet over and over with slight variations, I include it here for reference. Feel free to use or modify this assignment sheet for educational, non-commercial purposes.

Baseline Annotated Bibliography Assignment Sheet

Overview: In this assignment, you will create a 6-source annotated bibliography on a topic of your choice. Over the next 8 weeks you will work on your annotated bibliography bit by bit, and you will have the chance to incorporate feedback and revisions before submitting your completed annotated bibliography in week #9. This assignment is worth 50% of your course grade.
What is an Annotated Bibliography? Before answering this question, it makes sense to define "bibliography" and "annotation." A bibliography is a list of sources – books, articles, websites, and so on – that you cite in your work. An annotation is a type of note that describes, summarizes, evaluates, or reflects on a source. An "annotated bibliography" is, thus, a list of citations in which each citation is followed by an annotation directly below it. To see how your annotated bibliography should look, see the sample annotated bibliography at the end of this assignment sheet. [Attach a sample annotated bibliography].
Purpose of This Assignment: This assignment will reinforce the research and information literacy skills you learn in this course. In particular, your annotated bibliography will demonstrate that you have learned how to conduct college-level research and that you are able to appropriately select research sources. Students who work smarter (rather than harder) also use this annotated bibliography to help them find research sources for other courses. This is a very smart strategy!
Requirements: Your annotated bibliography will have the following features:

- It will be written in the *Google Docs* file that I will share with you. We will go over this in class.
- It will be written on a topic of your choice. Consider picking a topic that interests you or that you could use in other coursework. We will discuss your topic before you finalize it.
- It will contain an opening paragraph that briefly discusses why you picked your topic, what you hope to learn about your topic, and any preconceived notions you have about your topic. As an example: "I would like to research public health campaigns about the avian flu epidemic in the US, and it is my belief that not enough was done to inform

the public about the dangers of the virus. My mom got the avian flu, so I want to know what we could have done to prevent her from contracting the disease."
- It will contain 6 sources that you find in the library's catalog, in its databases, and on the web. We will learn about how to find and identify different types of sources in class.
- Each source in your annotated bibliography will have an annotation of 4–6 sentences. You will decide what information to highlight in this annotation, but ultimately you must convince me that your sources are a good fit with your topic. We will discuss how to assess the quality of your sources and how to write convincing annotations.
- It will follow the formatting guidelines modeled in the annotated bibliography included at the end of this assignment sheet. We will go over these formatting requirements in class.
- It will contain sources cited in whichever citation style you prefer. We will discuss strategies for citing sources.
- It will be submitted on [date]. I will accept late work for medical, legal, or compassionate reasons. I will *not* accept late work for reasons of forgetfulness, bad luck, or prioritizing other activities above this assignment.

Audience: I am the audience for your annotated bibliography. Assume I have a working knowledge of your topic and want to learn more. Do not assume I am an expert, however.

Assumptions: When writing your annotations, remember to focus on your topic and research question(s). Though you will not write a research paper in this course, pretending that you will write one (on your topic) will help you produce good annotations. Thus, when writing your annotations, consider how your research "fits" with your topic, and also consider how you could use your information when writing a paper. Thinking this way can help focus your annotated bibliography.

Rubric: [Always include a rubric with your assignment sheet. See rubrics in this chapter for options].

Sample Annotated Bibliography: [It helps students if you include a sample annotated bibliography with their assignment. See "Chapter #9: Three Sample Annotated Bibliographies" for samples.]

Assignment #1: The Simplest Annotated Bibliography

The Simplest Annotated Bibliography is a standard, meat-and-potatoes AB assignment. It requires students to produce a 6-source AB using a mix of popular and academic sources, and it obliges them to write an introductory paragraph explaining their topic and research question. Sources may be cited in whichever style the student chooses, though all sources must be cited with the same style. Students should write annotations briefly describing/summarizing their sources and justifying why they selected them. Students should pay particular attention to how appropriate their sources are for college-level research.

Subsequent assignments specify particular annotation writing requirements, but outside of length – 4–6 sentences should do – this assignment simply prompts students to justify why they selected their sources and tell you a little about them. How they do this is up to them. Give students a wide berth with their annotation writing, and as per the rubric, reward annotations that are lucid, substantive, and grammatically correct. Depending on the depth of your IL instruction, this assignment should take anywhere from 4 to 8 weeks.

Outcomes / Students Will...

- Produce a properly formatted AB.
- Produce reasonably correct bibliographic citations.
- Clearly articulate a topic/research question in an introductory paragraph.
- Select research sources appropriate to their topic.
- Annotate 6 sources in a manner consistent with assignment specifications.

Standards Alignment

Organization	Standards Alignment
Association of College & Research Library (ACRL) Standards	1.1; 1.2; 2.2; 3.1; 5.3
Association of College & Research Library (ACRL) Framework	Information Has Value; Research as Inquiry; Searching as Strategic Exploration
American Association of School Librarians (AASL) Learner Standards	Inquire A (Think) 1; Inquire B (Create) 1 & 3; Curate A (Think) 1–3; Curate B (Create) 4; Engage B (Create) 2
Association for American Colleges & Universities (AACU) Information Literacy VALUE Rubric	Determine the Extent of Information Needed; Access the Needed Information; Evaluate Information and its Sources Critically; Access and Use Information Ethically and Legally
International Federation of Library Associations & Institutions (IFLA) Guidelines for Lifelong Learning	A (Access) 1–2; B (Evaluation) 1–2
Society of College, National and University Libraries (SCONUL) Seven Pillars of Information Literacy	Scope; Plan; Gather; Evaluation; Manage

Baseline Assignment Sheet Changes

- Uses baseline assignment sheet without any changes.

Teaching Notes

- Popular and scholarly source differentiation is important for this assignment. Ensure you emphasize these differences early and often in your IL instruction.
- By design, this assignment does not prescribe specific annotation writing guidelines other than length. Let students know, however, that their annotations must be clear and that they should justify their source selections in light of their topic and research question(s).
- This assignment is meant to be forgiving, so go easy on the grading with the exception of assignment formatting (which is often a proxy for how much effort students put into their work).

Suggested Rubric

	Proficient (A)	Satisfactory (B)	Developing (C)	Inadequate (F)
Introductory Paragraph	Introductory paragraph is present. Text is expertly written, and research question is well-formulated.	Introductory paragraph is present. Text is competently written, and research question is articulated.	Introductory paragraph is present. Text is indifferently written, and research question is vague or overly broad.	Introductory paragraph is absent or nonsensical. Does not articulate a research question or research interest.
Source Quality	Found correct number and type of sources. Sources highly related to topic and display considerable expertise.	Found correct number and type of sources. Sources related to topic, with most displaying expertise.	Found correct number and type of sources. Sources related to topic, though may lack a degree of expertise.	Did not find correct number or type of sources OR sources are irrelevant or only loosely related to topic.
Annotation Quality	Annotation conforms to specified length. Annotations are very well-written, and fully capture the essence of sources.	Annotation conforms to specified length. Annotations are generally well-written, and adequately capture the essence of sources.	Annotation conforms to specified length. Annotations are coherent, and somewhat capture the essence of sources.	Annotation does not conform to specified length OR annotations are incoherent or inadequately capture the essence of sources.
Citations	Citations are entirely error-free. Formatting is correct.	Citations contain very few errors. Formatting is correct.	Citations contain some errors. Formatting is mostly correct.	Citations are absent or contain many errors. Formatting is incorrect.
Formatting	Annotated bibliography formatting conforms to assignment requirements with no errors.	Annotated bibliography formatting largely conforms to assignment requirements with only 1–2 errors.	Annotated bibliography formatting mostly conforms to assignment requirements with occasional errors.	Annotated bibliography formatting does not conform to assignment requirements or is largely incorrect.

Further Reading

For additional readings about basic AB assignments, see the following in the Further Reading section at the end of this chapter: Birkett and Hughes (2013); Brinkman and Hartsell-Gundy (2012); Edwards and Black (2012); Fitzpatrick and Costley (2017); Koss (2014); Lidzy (2010/2011); Mackey (2004); Mostert and Townsend (2018); and Tan-de Ramos (2015).

Assignment #2: Annotated Bibliography with Different Source Types

In this assignment, students will produce an 8-source AB. The AB will include an introductory paragraph outlining their topic and research question. Students will find 3 academic articles, 3 books or book chapters, 1 web resource, and 1 video addressing their topic. Their sources should provide varied perspectives on their topic. Sources may be cited in whichever style the student chooses, though all sources should be cited in the same style. Annotations will be 6–8 sentences, and will discuss source format, authorship, main idea(s), and pertinence to the student's topic and research question. Students should end their annotations by identifying the source type and whether it is academic or popular.

Identifying source types is a particular point of emphasis in this assignment. For many first-year students, the differences between, say, a book chapter and an academic article might well be mystagogic. This assignment forces a degree of clarity on the matter and helps students learn about how source types *actually* differ. Like the first assignment, annotation writing is a largely unstructured affair, with students recording basic descriptive and summative information about their sources, followed by a brief justification of why they selected them. Annotations of 6–8 sentences should get the job done, and lucid, grammatically correct annotations should be rewarded. Depending on the depth of your IL instruction, the assignment should take 5–10 weeks.

Outcomes / Students Will...

- Produce a properly formatted AB.
- Produce reasonably correct bibliographic citations.
- Select research sources appropriate to the student's topic and research question.
- Select correct number and type of sources, as specified in assignment instructions.
- Write effective annotations for each source.

Standards Alignment

Organization	Standards Alignment
Association of College & Research Library (ACRL) Standards	1.1; 1.2; 2.2; 2.5; 3.1; 5.3
Association of College & Research Library (ACRL) Framework	Information Has Value; Research as Inquiry; Searching as Strategic Exploration
American Association of School Librarians (AASL) Learner Standards	Inquire A (Think) 1; Inquire B (Create) 1 & 3; Include A (Think) 2; Curate A (Think) 1–3; Curate B (Create) 1 & 4; Explore A (Think) 1; Engage B (Create) 2
Association for American Colleges & Universities (AACU) Information Literacy VALUE Rubric	Determine the Extent of Information Needed; Access the Needed Information; Evaluate Information and its Sources Critically; Access and Use Information Ethically and Legally
International Federation of Library Associations & Institutions (IFLA) Guidelines for Lifelong Learning	A (Access) 1–2; B (Evaluation) 1–2
Society of College, National and University Libraries (SCONUL) Seven Pillars of Information Literacy	Scope; Plan; Gather; Evaluate; Manage

Baseline Assignment Sheet Changes

- AB requires 8 sources, including 3 books or book chapters, 3 academic articles, 1 web resource, and 1 video.
- AB requires annotations of 6–8 sentences for each source. The annotations will contain information about the source's format, authorship, main idea(s), and pertinence to the student's topic and research question.

Teaching Notes

- First-year undergraduate students are notoriously poor at differentiating source formats. This tendency is frustrating for librarians, but also understandable given that information sources at the secondary level are mostly textbooks and primary sources. Ensure your IL instruction is thorough when it comes to identifying source formats.
- Identifying online source formats is also vexing for students, so attune your instruction accordingly.
- Requiring a video source will push students a little, but affords you the opportunity to teach about the differences between professional and amateur video. If your campus subscribes to a streaming video platform (e.g., *Kanopy*, *Swank*), you can note that these platforms carry more reputable content than is typically found on tube sites.

Suggested Rubric

	Exemplary	Satisfactory	Unsatisfactory
Variety of Sources	Found the required number and type of sources. Sources fully address differing and credible perspectives on the topic.	Found the required number and type of sources. Sources address differing and credible perspective on the topic.	Did not find the required number and/or type of sources OR sources address only a single perspective on the topic.
Academic Sources	Found the required number and/or type of academic sources. All sources have a clear and significant relationship to the topic.	Found the required number and/or type of academic sources. Most sources have a clear and significant relationship to the topic.	Did not find the required number and/or type of academic sources OR sources do not relate or relate only tangentially to the topic.
Popular Sources	Found the required number and/or type of popular sources. Sources appear to have undergone thorough vetting, and were likely chosen from an array of viable alternatives.	Found the required number and/or type of popular sources. Sources appear to have undergone some vetting, and were likely chosen from at least some alternatives.	Did not find the required number and/or type of popular sources OR sources appear indifferently chosen and were likely taken from the first page of a hurried Google search.
Annotation Quality	Annotation conforms to specified length. Annotations are very well-written and fully capture the essence of sources.	Annotation conforms to specified length. Annotations are capably written and capture the essence of sources.	Annotation does not conform to specified length OR annotations are incoherent or inadequately capture the essence of sources.
Citations & Formatting	Citations are entirely error-free. Citation and assignment formatting are consistent and correct.	Citations contain a few, small errors. Citation and assignment formatting are consistent and correct.	Citations are absent or contain frequent errors. Citation and assignment formatting are inconsistent or incorrect.

Further Reading

For additional readings about AB assignments using different source types, see the following in the Further Reading section at the end of this chapter: Callas (2010); Daugman et al. (2012); Diamond (2019); Faix (2014); Flaspohler et al. (2007); Guise et al. (2008); Laskin and Haller (2017); Leigh and Gibbon (2008); Luckman (2009); Mackey and Jacobson (2004); Mounce (2006); and Mounce (2013).

Assignment #3: Annotated Bibliography with Combined Annotations

In this assignment, students will produce a 6-source AB on a topic of their choice, wherein each of their annotations will be written with some combination of the descriptive, summative, evaluative, and reflective annotation types outlined in "Chapter #3: Teaching Annotation Types." Students can include a mix of popular and academic sources in their ABs, but should be encouraged to lean more heavily on academic sources (say, 4 out 6). Students may cite sources in whichever style they prefer, with all sources cited in the same style. Depending on the depth of your IL instruction, the assignment should take 6–10 weeks.

Total annotation length should range from 6–10 sentences. Indicate to students that a suggested length for each annotation element might look something like the following...

- Descriptive elements = 1–2 sentences
- Summative elements = 2–4 sentences
- Evaluative elements = 1–3 sentences
- Reflective elements = 1–2 sentences

... and indicate to students that they must include three or more of the listed annotation elements in each of their combined annotations. Because annotation writing is trickier here than in the previous two assignments, consider an assignment schedule that allows for sufficient writing time. I recommend giving students at least 2 weeks to write and refine their annotations. Remember to emphasize that students should justify why they selected their sources. Students should also pay particular attention to how appropriate their sources are for college-level research.

Outcomes / Students Will...

- Produce a properly formatted AB.
- Produce reasonably correct bibliographic citations.
- Select sources appropriate to their topic.
- Annotate sources using a combination of descriptive, summative, evaluative, and reflective elements.

Standards Alignment

Organization	Standards Alignment
Association of College & Research Library (ACRL) Standards	1.1; 1.2; 1.4; 2.2; 3.1; 3.2; 3.4; 3.5; 5.3
Association of College & Research Library (ACRL) Framework	Information Has Value; Research as Inquiry; Scholarship as Conversation; Searching as Strategic Exploration
American Association of School Librarians (AASL) Learner Standards	Inquire A (Think) 1; Inquire B (Create) 1 & 3; Include A (Think) 2; Curate A (Think) 1–3; Curate B (Create) 3–4; Curate D (Grow) 1; Engage A (Think) 3; Engage B (Create) 2
Association for American Colleges & Universities (AACU) Information Literacy VALUE Rubric	Determine the Extent of Information Needed; Access the Needed Information; Evaluate Information and its Sources Critically; Access and Use Information Ethically and Legally
International Federation of Library Associations & Institutions (IFLA) Guidelines for Lifelong Learning	A (Access) 1–2; B (Evaluation) 1–2
Society of College, National and University Libraries (SCONUL) Seven Pillars of Information Literacy	Scope; Plan; Gather; Evaluation; Manage

Baseline Assignment Sheet Changes

- AB annotations will be 6–10 sentences. Each annotation will contain any three of the following: a descriptive element between 1–2 sentences; a summative element between 2–4 sentences; an evaluative element between 1–3 sentences; or a reflective element between 1–2 sentences.
- Students will color their descriptive elements blue, their summative elements green, their evaluative elements red, and their reflective elements black. They will do this so you can easily identify which annotative elements they are using.

- There is no introductory paragraph in this assignment required, owing to the complexity of writing combined annotations. Students should still clear their topic with you before beginning their research.

Teaching Notes

- You will need to teach the descriptive, summative, evaluative, and reflective annotation types. Having students master these annotation types will allow them to capture the essence of their sources.
- Research has shown that undergraduate students are often poor at evaluating sources. Prepare to be underwhelmed – and grade accordingly – when students' evaluative and reflective annotation elements do not meaningfully engage with their sources.
- Identifying high-quality sources will put students in a better position to write more substantive annotations. For this assignment, ensure your source evaluation lessons are sharp!
- When writing reflective annotation elements, students must consider their research question or topic. How does a given source contribute to answering their question? How does a given source fit with other sources? The class can generate additional questions to guide reflective annotations.

Suggested Rubric

	Exceeds Expectations (A)	Standards Met (B)	Standards Partially Met (C)	Standards Not Met (F)
Descriptive & Summative Annotation Elements	Annotations conform to specified length. They artfully, succinctly, and accurately describe material and summarize key elements/arguments.	Annotations conform to specified length. They accurately describe material and summarize key elements/arguments.	Annotations mostly conform to specified length. They passably describe material and summarize key elements/arguments.	Annotations largely do not conform to specified length OR they fail to describe material or summarize key elements/arguments.
Evaluative Annotation Elements	Annotations conform to specified length. They evaluate/critique the material with insight and genuine engagement.	Annotations conform to specified length. They evaluate/critique the material with a degree of thought and care.	Annotations mostly conform to specified length. They indifferently evaluate/critique the material.	Annotations largely do not conform to specified length OR they make no attempt to evaluate or critique the material.

(Continued)

	Exceeds Expectations (A)	Standards Met (B)	Standards Partially Met (C)	Standards Not Met (F)
Reflective Annotation Elements	Annotations conform to specified length. They thoughtfully account for why the material was selected and how it supports the topic.	Annotations conform to specified length. They adequately account for why the material was selected and how it supports the topic	Annotations mostly conform to specified length. They make token efforts to justify why the material was selected and how it supports the topic.	Annotations do not conform to specified length OR they make no attempt to justify why the material was selected.
Source Quality	Found correct number and type of sources. Sources highly related to topic and display considerable expertise.	Found correct number and type of sources. Sources are related to topic, with most displaying expertise.	Found correct number and type of sources. Sources related to topic, though may lack a degree of expertise.	Did not find correct number or type of sources OR sources are irrelevant or only loosely related to topic.
Citations & Formatting	Citations are entirely error-free. AB formatting is correct.	Citations contain very few errors. AB formatting has minor errors.	Citations contain some errors. AB formatting has some errors.	Citations are absent or contain many errors, AND AB formatting is mostly incorrect.

Further Reading

For additional readings about AB assignments using fully developed annotations, see the following in the Further Reading section at the end of this chapter: Bobkowski and Younger (2020); Hoffmann and LaBonte (2012); Jensen (2017); Koss (2014); Lidzy (2010/2011); Mussleman and Bucker (2012); Paglia and Donohue (2003); Risanti (2019); Spires et al. (2019); and Whatley (2006).

Assignment #4: Source Evaluation Annotated Bibliography

In this assignment, students will write an 8-source AB. The AB will include an introductory paragraph outlining the student's topic and research question. Like most AB assignments, students will find a mix of academic and popular sources, and produce citations and annotations. Their sources should provide varied perspectives on their topic. In this version of the AB, students write their annotations by explicitly drawing on source evaluation methods taught in the course. For example, if your source evaluation lessons teach the CRAAB method, students should write annotations that address each letter of CRAAB in 1–2 sentences. Here are some source evaluation methods/acronyms you might use:

- CRAAB = Currency, Relevance, Authority, Accuracy, Bias.
- PROVEN = Purpose, Relevance, Objectivity, Verifiability, Expertise, Newness.
- PAACE = Purpose, Authority, Accuracy, Currency, Ease of Use.
- RAVEN = Reputation, Ability to observe, Vested interest, Expertise, Neutrality.
- SIFT = Stop, Investigate claims, Find better coverage, Trace claims.
- 5 Ws = Who?, What?, Where?, When?, Why?
- CRITIC = Claim, Role of claimant, Information backing claim, Testing, Independent verification, Conclusion.
- Other source evaluation methods not using acronyms.

Depending on your chosen method of source evaluation, student annotations should be between six and eight sentences. As with any annotations, ensure students have sufficiently justified their source selection vis-à-vis their topic and research question. As with other AB assignments, allow students to cite using their chosen style, provided they are consistent across their citations. This is a good assignment for librarians who lean heavily into source evaluation in their IL instruction. Depending on the depth of your IL instruction, the assignment should take 5–10 weeks.

Outcomes / Students Will...

- Produce a properly formatted AB.
- Produce reasonably correct bibliographic citations.

- Clearly articulate a topic and researchable question in an introductory paragraph.
- Select research sources appropriate to topic.
- Annotate 8 sources with reference to the method(s) of source evaluation taught in the course.

Standards Alignment

Organization	Standards Alignment
Association of College & Research Library (ACRL) Standards	1.1; 1.2; 1.4; 2.2; 2.5; 3.2; 5.3
Association of College & Research Library (ACRL) Framework	Authority is Constructed and Contextual; Information Has Value; Research as Inquiry; Searching as Strategic Exploration
American Association of School Librarians (AASL) Learner Standards	Inquire A (Think) 1; Inquire B (Create) 1 & 3; Include A (Think) 2; Curate A (Think) 1–3; Curate B (Create) 1 & 3; Curate D (Grow) 1; Engage A (Think) 3; Engage B (Create) 2
Association for American Colleges & Universities (AACU) Information Literacy VALUE Rubric	Determine the Extent of Information Needed; Access the Needed Information; Evaluate Information and its Sources Critically; Access and Use Information Ethically and Legally
International Federation of Library Associations & Institutions (IFLA) Guidelines for Lifelong Learning	A (Access) 1–2; B (Evaluation) 1–2
Society of College, National and University Libraries (SCONUL) Seven Pillars of Information Literacy	Scope; Plan; Gather; Evaluate; Manage

Baseline Assignment Sheet Changes

- AB requires 8 sources. Can be a mix of academic and popular sources.
- AB requires annotations of 6–8 sentences for each source. In writing annotations, students must explicitly use the source evaluation method(s) taught in the course.

Teaching Notes

- Many (perhaps most) librarians have reservations about using acronym-based methods to teach source evaluation. If you use an acronym-based method, pick one that you can completely get behind. Students will sniff out ambivalence!
- Annotations may not flow as smoothly as they otherwise would because of the possible constraints of the evaluation method. Grade annotations on content, not style, artfulness, or other such traits.
- Talk with students about the introductory paragraph. Model a few good ones. Do not let students get away with variations of the sentence, "My topic is x and I'm interested in it and I would like to learn more." Force a degree of specificity on the students.

Suggested Rubric

Areas for Improvement	Criteria	Meets or Exceeds Expectations
[comments]	*Introductory Paragraph:* Introductory paragraph is present and outlines topic and research question.	[comments]
	Sources: Found correct number and type of sources. Sources address different aspects of topic.	
	Citations & Formatting: Citations and assignment formatting are correct. Errors kept to a minimum.	

(Continued)

Areas for Improvement	Criteria	Meets or Exceeds Expectations
	*C*urrency: Publication date for sources is noted, evaluated, and appropriate for topic.	
	*R*elevance: Annotation evaluates whether sources are clearly and substantially related to topic.	
	*A*uthority: Annotation identifies author(s) and/or organization(s) and their expertise.	
	*A*ccuracy: Annotation reviews evidence, references, hyperlinks, etc., used to support claims.	
	*B*ias(es): Source bias, if present, is identified and reflected on.	

Further Reading

For additional readings about AB assignments emphasizing source evaluation, see the following in the Further Reading section at the end of this chapter: Belanger et al. (2015); Carbery and Leahy (2015); Engeldinger (1988); Gauder and Jenkins (2012); King (2010); Mills et al. (2021); Pashaie (2009); Rinto (2013); and Rinto and Cogbill-Seiders (2015).

Assignment #5: Visual Annotated Bibliography

In this assignment, students will write an 8-source AB with an introductory paragraph outlining their topic and research question. Students will construct their ABs in *Excel* or *Google Sheets*. Doing this will allow students to compartmentalize information about their sources and learn a visual organizational strategy for tracking research. I recommend setting up a sheet to share with students. The sheet should, at the very least, title, have columns for permalinks, source types, a popular/academic categorization, citations, and annotations. See below for an example of how this might look:

Source Title	Permalink	Source Type	Popular / Academic	Citation	Annotation
Title	[URL]	Book	Academic	[citation]	[annotation]

In gathering sources, students will select 2–3 books or book chapters, 2–3 academic articles, and 2–3 sources of their choice. The sources may be popular and academic, and students should identify them as such in their *Excel* or *Google Sheets* file. Their sources should provide varied perspectives on their topic. Annotations should range between 4–6 sentences, identify key source features, and explain how the source connects to the student's topic. You should give students a wide berth with their annotation writing, but emphasize that you expect lucid and grammatically correct annotations. Students should consult with you before settling on a topic. Depending on the depth of your IL instruction, this assignment should take 6–10 weeks.

Outcomes / Students Will...

- Produce a properly formatted AB.
- Produce reasonably correct bibliographic citations.
- Clearly articulate a topic and researchable question in an introductory paragraph.
- Select sources appropriate to their topic.
- Learn why permalinks/stable URLs are important.
- Annotate 8 research sources in a manner consistent with assignment specifications.

Librarian Assignments   119

- Sufficiently master *Excel* or *Google Sheets* such that the assignment is completed and submitted without undue librarian intervention.

Standards Alignment

Organization	Standards Alignment
Association of College & Research Library (ACRL) Standards	1.1; 1.2; 2.2; 2.5; 3.1; 3.3; 4.1; 5.3
Association of College & Research Library (ACRL) Framework	Information Has Value; Research as Inquiry; Searching as Strategic Exploration
American Association of School Librarians (AASL) Learner Standards	Inquire A (Think) 1; Inquire B (Create) 1 & 3; Collaborate B (Create) 1; Curate A (Think) 1–3; Curate B (Create) 4; Engage A (Think) 3; Engage B (Create) 2
Association for American Colleges & Universities (AACU) Information Literacy VALUE Rubric	Determine the Extent of Information Needed; Access the Needed Information; Evaluate Information and its Sources Critically; Access and Use Information Ethically and Legally
International Federation of Library Associations & Institutions (IFLA) Guidelines for Lifelong Learning	A (Access) 1–2; B (Evaluation) 1–2; C (Use) 1
Society of College, National and University Libraries (SCONUL) Seven Pillars of Information Literacy	Scope; Plan; Gather; Evaluate; Manage

Baseline Assignment Sheet Changes

- Students will write ABs in *Excel* or *Google Sheets* (or potentially other products, like *Zotero*). The librarian will share the *Excel* or *Google Sheets* file with the student. Students will need an example of how this process works, and assignment sheet should include this information in the "Requirements" section.

- AB will contain (8) sources, including (2–3) books or book chapters, (2–3) academic articles, and (2–3) sources of the student's choice.
- If needed, students invest time mastering *Excel* or *Google Sheets*, such that their ABs are written and submitted without undue librarian intervention.

Teaching Notes

- Provide a dedicated cell in the *Excel* or *Google Sheets* file for students to include their introductory paragraphs.
- Citations will not have a hanging indentation, because indenting in cells is difficult. Remind students that in other contexts they will most likely need to produce citations with hanging indentations.
- Your IL lessons should have the popular vs. academic discussion early in your teaching sequence.
- Ensure you explain permalinks/stable URLs early in your teaching sequence. If students fail to master permalinks/stable URLs, they will have difficulty finding their sources again.
- This assignment is more explicitly recursive than other AB assignments, in that students will venture back to their sheets repeatedly to fill them in with new and additional information.
- If an *Excel* or *Google Sheets* file seems a little staid, consider having students produce their ABs in another visual form, such as concept maps, infographics, or charts. This puts an additional technical burden on students, but can add verve to the assignment.

Suggested Rubric

Areas for Improvement	Criteria	Meets or Exceeds Expectations
[comments]	*Introductory Paragraph:* Introductory paragraph is present, cogent, and explains topic and research question.	[comments]

(Continued)

Areas for Improvement	Criteria	Meets or Exceeds Expectations
	Sources: Found correct number and type of sources. Sources address differing aspects of topic.	
	Citations: Citations are correctly styled and consistently. Permalinks/URLs work.	
	Annotation Quality: Annotations conform to specified length, capture the essence of sources, identify source types, and tell how sources support topic.	
	Tech Savvy: Student effectively uses the provided Excel or Google Sheets template. Student invests the necessary time to master the product.	

Further Reading

For additional readings about visual AB assignments similar to this one, see the following in the Further Reading section at the end of this chapter: Amin (2011); Lunsford (2015); Goodman et al. (2018); Knox et al. (2019); Martelo (2011); Richards (2015); Sample (2011); Sharif (2017); Spires et al. (2019); and Winslow et al. (2017).

Assignment #6: Group Annotated Bibliography

In this assignment, students will work in groups of 3 to produce a 14-source AB on a topic of their choice. Students will write their annotations using some combination of the descriptive, summative, evaluative, and reflective annotation types outlined in "Chapter #3: Teaching Annotation Types." In addition, the AB will include an introductory paragraph outlining the group's topic, research question(s), and how each group member will contribute to the project. Prior to beginning their research, groups must meet with you in order to clear their topic and establish their work roles. After finishing their ABs, group members will evaluate their fellow group members' contributions.

In gathering their 14 sources, students will select 3–6 books or book chapters, 3–6 academic articles, and 3–6 sources of their choice. The sources may be both popular and academic and should provide varied perspectives on the group's topic. Annotations should average between 6–8 sentences. The breakdown of annotations should roughly be as follows…

- Descriptive elements = 1–2 sentences
- Summative elements = 2–4 sentences
- Evaluative elements = 1–3 sentences
- Reflective elements = 1–2 sentences

… and sources should be consistently cited in whichever style the group elects. Depending on the depth of your IL instruction, the assignment should take 7–10 weeks to complete.

Outcomes / Students Will…

- Produce a properly formatted AB.
- Produce reasonably correct bibliographic citations.
- Clearly articulate a topic, research question, and group member roles in an introductory paragraph.
- Select research sources appropriate to the group's topic.
- Annotate 14 sources in a manner consistent with assignment specifications.
- Work effectively with group members (including peer evaluation).

Standards Alignment

Organization	Standards Alignment
Association of College & Research Library (ACRL) Standards	1.1; 1.2; 2.2; 3.1; 3.6; 4.3; 5.3
Association of College & Research Library (ACRL) Framework	Information Has Value; Research as Inquiry; Scholarship as Conversation; Searching as Strategic Exploration
American Association of School Librarians (AASL) Learner Standards	Inquire A (Think) 1; Inquire B (Create) 1 & 3; Inquire C (Share) 1; Include B (Create) 1; Collaborate A (Think) 2–3; Collaborate C (Share) 1; Collaborate D (Grow) 1–2; Curate A (Think) 1–3; Curate B (Create) 4; Curate C (Share) 1–3; Engage B (Create) 2
Association for American Colleges & Universities (AACU) Information Literacy VALUE Rubric	Determine the Extent of Information Needed; Access the Needed Information; Evaluate Information and its Sources Critically; Access and Use Information Ethically and Legally
International Federation of Library Associations & Institutions (IFLA) Guidelines for Lifelong Learning	A (Access) 1–2; B (Evaluation) 1–2
Society of College, National and University Libraries (SCONUL) Seven Pillars of Information Literacy	Scope; Plan; Gather; Evaluate; Manage

Baseline Assignment Sheet Changes

- Specify how many students should be in a group. Three seems reasonable.
- AB will contain 14 total sources, including 3–6 books or book chapters, 3–6 academic articles, and 3–6 sources of the group's choice.

- AB will contain annotations of 6–8 sentences. Each annotation will be written with 3 or more of the following annotative elements: descriptive (1–2 sentences); summative (2–4 sentences); evaluative (1–3 sentences); or reflective (1–2 sentences).
- Students will color their descriptive elements blue, their summative elements green, their evaluative elements red, and their reflective elements black. They will do this so you can easily identify which annotative elements they are using.
- Because this involves groupwork, the assignment should be less than 50% of the course grade.
- Introductory paragraph must specify each group members' duties.

Teaching Notes

- Consider assigning groups rather than letting students self-select.
- Though pedagogically useful, group assignments have a lot of moving parts and can be a pain for both instructors and students. Given this, I would not deploy this assignment for remedial or developmental classes.
- When initially negotiating group roles, ensure each student has something significant to do in each stage of the assignment. For example, all students should contribute to finding resources, writing annotations, producing and/or double-checking citations, and so on.
- When doing check-ins, insist on meeting with the group together. Meeting with individual group members can lead to dropped or garbled communication.
- Individuals should receive their own grades. Peer review of one another's contributions will somewhat affect the grade.

Suggested Rubric

	Exemplary (A)	Satisfactory (B–C)	Unsatisfactory (D–F)
Introductory Paragraph	Introductory paragraph is present. Text is expertly written, and research question is well-formulated. Group member responsibilities are outlined, and workload is evenly distributed.	Introductory paragraph is present. Text is competently written, and research question is articulated. Group member responsibilities are outlined, and workload is more or less fair.	Introductory paragraph is absent or nonsensical. It does not articulate a research question or research interest. Group member responsibilities are vague or unstated.
Variety of Sources	Found the required number and type of sources. Sources address differing and credible perspectives on topic.	Found the required number and type of sources. Sources address more than one aspect of topic and most are credible.	Did not find the required number and/or type of sources OR sources are mostly of low quality.
Annotation Quality	Annotations conform to specified length. Annotations are very well-written and fully capture the essence of sources. Descriptive, summative, evaluative, and/or reflective elements are used well.	Annotations conform to specified length. Annotations are capably written and adequately capture the essence of sources. Some of the descriptive, summative, evaluative, and/or reflective elements are present.	Annotations do not conform to specified length. Annotations are incoherent or inadequately capture the essence of sources. Descriptive, summative, evaluative, and/or reflective elements are lacking.
Citations & Formatting	Citations are entirely error-free. AB formatting is entirely consistent and correct.	Citations contain a few, small errors. AB formatting is largely consistent and correct.	Citations are absent or contain frequent errors. AB formatting is inconsistent or incorrect.
Engagement	In peer review, group members indicate student made significant contributions to the project.	In peer review, group members indicate student made reasonable contributions to the project.	In peer review, group members indicate student made minimal contributions to the project.

Further Reading

For additional readings about group AB assignments similar to this one, see the following in the Further Reading section at the end of this chapter: Charles and DeFabiis (2021); Croft et al. (2019); Finch and Jefferson (2013); King-O'Brien et al. (2021); Muñoz (2012); Parkes et al. (2013); Patterson (2011); Winicki (2006); and Zanin-Yost (2018).

Assignment #7: Scaffolded Annotated Bibliography

In this assignment, students will produce an AB and use it to write a subsequent research paper. (This section describes the AB assignment, not the research paper.) Students will find 6 sources, including 2 books or book chapters, 2 academic articles, and 2 sources of their choice. The students will then annotate their sources with basic descriptive and summative information. Following that, they will evaluate source quality and reflect on how the sources will support their upcoming research paper. In addition, students will write an introductory paragraph that outlines their topic, research question, and a potential thesis for their paper. Topics will be discussed with the librarian before the student begins their research in earnest.

Sources may be cited in whichever style the student chooses, though all sources should be cited in the same style. Annotations should be kept brisk – no more than 6 sentences – and the assignment should take no more than 8 weeks in light of the subsequent research paper assignment. Given that reflective annotation elements feature heavily in this assignment, ensure students are comfortable with how to write them. Also, remind students that while their ABs will help with their research papers, their research will be ongoing – arguments evolve, theses change, new interests arise, and so on. To support these shifts in direction, students will most likely need new research.

Outcomes / Students Will...

- Produce a properly formatted AB.
- Produce reasonably correct bibliographic citations.
- Clearly articulate a topic, researchable question, and potential thesis in an introductory paragraph.
- Select research sources appropriate to their topic.
- Annotate 6 sources in a manner consistent with assignment specifications.
- Use their AB to support a subsequent research paper.

Standards Alignment

Organization	Standards Alignment
Association of College & Research Library (ACRL) Standards	1.1; 1.2; 1.4; 2.2; 3.1; 3.7; 5.3
Association of College & Research Library (ACRL) Framework	Information Has Value; Research as Inquiry; Searching as Strategic Exploration
American Association of School Librarians (AASL) Learner Standards	Inquire A (Think) 1; Inquire B (Create) 1 & 3; Inquire C (Share) 3; Curate A (Think) 1–3; Curate B (Create) 1; Explore C (Share) 1; Engage A (Think) 3; Engage B (Create) 2
Association for American Colleges & Universities (AACU) Information Literacy VALUE Rubric	Determine the Extent of Information Needed; Access the Needed Information; Evaluate Information and its Sources Critically; Access and Use Information Ethically and Legally
International Federation of Library Associations & Institutions (IFLA) Guidelines for Lifelong Learning	A (Access) 1–2; B (Evaluation) 1–2
Society of College, National and University Libraries (SCONUL) Seven Pillars of Information Literacy	Scope; Plan; Gather; Evaluate; Manage

Baseline Assignment Sheet Changes

- AB requires 6 sources, including 2 books or book chapters, 2 academic articles, and 2 sources of the student's choice.
- AB requires annotations of 6 sentences for each source. The annotations will contain basic descriptive and summative information. Annotations will also evaluate source quality and reflect on how the sources will support their upcoming research paper.

- The "Assumptions" section should be revised, because students are writing ABs to support a research paper. This revision should emphasize how sources will address the student's topic, research question, or potential thesis.
- Assignment should be worth 30–40% of course grade.

Teaching Notes

- Though students should write fairly structured annotations, pay particular attention to their reflective elements. The reflective elements will provide the clearest evidence that students are *actually* thinking about their upcoming papers.
- As the AB plays second fiddle to a research paper in this assignment sequence, I recommend going easy with your AB grading. At first glance, the rubric seems stringent, but interpret it generously and keep students buoyed for their research papers.
- Given that you (probably) are not a writing instructor, a shorter research paper is in order. No need to put yourself in an early grave!
- If you are co-teaching an IL class with a composition or WAC instructor, your focus should mostly be on the AB. Let the other instructor handle the research paper.
- When used as a scaffolding tool, the AB most commonly supports research papers, though examples in the literature also include posters, presentations, speeches, podcasts, and other types of assignments. If the research paper is not to your taste, consider something more contemporary.

Suggested Rubric

	Proficient (A)	Satisfactory (B)	Developing (C)	Inadequate (F)
Introductory Paragraph	Introductory paragraph is present. Text is expertly written and research question is well-formulated.	Introductory paragraph is present. Text is competently written, and research question is articulated.	Introductory paragraph is present. Text is indifferently written, and research question is vague or overly broad.	Introductory paragraph is absent or nonsensical OR does not articulate a research question.
Annotation Quality	Annotations conform to specified length. Annotations are very well-written and fully capture the essence of sources.	Annotations conform to specified length. Annotations are well-written and adequately capture the essence of sources.	Annotations conform to specified length. Annotations are coherent and somewhat capture the essence of sources.	Annotations do not conform to specified length OR annotations are incoherent or inadequately capture the essence of sources.
Reflective Annotation Element	Annotations thoughtfully address why sources were chosen and how they will/might be used in the research paper.	Annotations address why sources were chosen and how they will/might be used in the research paper.	Annotations speciously address why sources were chosen and how they will/might be used in the research paper.	Annotations do not address why sources were chosen or how they will/might be used in the research paper.
Source Quality	Found correct number and type of sources. Sources highly relate to topic and display considerable expertise.	Found correct number and type of sources. Sources relate to topic, with most displaying expertise.	Found correct number and type of sources. Sources relate to topic, though may lack a degree of expertise.	Did not find correct number or type of sources OR sources are irrelevant or only loosely related to topic.
Citations & Formatting	Citations are entirely error-free. AB formatting is correct.	Citations contain very few errors. AB formatting is mostly correct.	Citations contain several errors. AB formatting is mostly correct.	Citations are absent or contain frequent errors. Assignment formatting is incorrect.

Further Reading

For additional readings about scaffolded AB assignments similar to this one, see the following in the Further Reading section at the end of this chapter: Armstrong and Fast (2004); Flaspohler et al. (2007); Franzen and Bannon (2016); Goodman et al. (2018); Hosier (2015); Inusa et al. (2018); Jones (2010); Knox et al. (2019); Lantz (2016); Laskin and Haller (2017); Luckman (2009); Mazella et al. (2011); Quezada (2016); Rose-Wiles et al. (2017); Russom (2003); Spires et al. (2019); Sternadel (2004); and Zanin-Yost (2018).

Further Reading

American Association of School Librarians. *Standards Crosswalks.* American Library Association, 2021, https://is.gd/02Cdox.

Amin, Latifah, et al. "Enhancing Biotechnology Education through Annotated Bibliographies." *Procedia - Social and Behavioral Sciences*, vol. 15, 2011, pp. 3389–93, https://doi.org/10.1016/j.sbspro.2011.04.306.

Armstrong, Jeanne, and Margaret Fast. "A Credit Course Assignment: The Encyclopedia Entry." *Reference Services Review*, vol. 32, no. 2, 2004, pp. 190–94, https://doi.org/10.1108/00907320410537711.

Association of American Colleges & Universities. *Information Literacy VALUE Rubric.* Association of American Colleges & Universities, 2017, https://is.gd/FFEHLW.

Association of College and Research Libraries. *Framework for Information Literacy for Higher Education.* American Library Association, 2016, https://is.gd/RSmGkY.

Association of College and Research Libraries. *Information Literacy Competency Standards for Higher Education.* American Library Association, 2000, https://is.gd/69WGsM.

Belanger, Jackie, et al. "Project RAILS: Lessons Learned about Rubric Assessment of Information Literacy Skills." *Portal: Libraries and the Academy*, vol. 15, no. 4, 2015, pp. 623–44, https://doi.org/10.1353/pla.2015.0050.

Birkett, Melissa, and Amy Hughes. "A Collaborative Project to Integrate Information Literacy Skills into an Undergraduate Psychology Course." *Psychology Learning & Teaching*, vol. 12, no. 1, 2013, pp. 96–100, https://doi.org/10.2304/plat.2013.12.1.96.

Bobkowski, Piotr S., and Karna Younger. "News Credibility: Adapting and Testing a Source Evaluation Assessment in Journalism." *College & Research Libraries*, vol. 81, no. 5, 2020, pp. 822–43, https://doi.org/10.5860/crl.81.5.822.

Brinkman, Stacy N., and Arianne A. Hartsell-Gundy. "Building Trust to Relieve Graduate Student Research Anxiety." *Public Services Quarterly*,

vol. 8, no. 1, 2012, pp. 26–39, https://doi.org/10.1080/15228959.2011.591680.
Callas, Jennie E. "Assessing One-Shot Instruction: Using Post-Assignment Evaluations to Build Better Assignments." *Thirty-Sixth National LOEX Library Instruction Conference Proceedings: Librarian as Architect: Planning, Building, & Renewing*, edited by Brad Sietz, LOEX Press, 2010, pp. 35–39, https://is.gd/0BK2LE.
Carbery, Alan, and Sean Leahy. "Evidence-Based Instruction: Assessing Student Work Using Rubrics and Citation Analysis to Inform Instructional Design." *Journal of Information Literacy*, vol. 9, no. 1, 2015, pp. 74–90, https://doi.org/10.11645/9.1.1980.
Carey, Ellen. *P.R.O.V.E.N. Source Evaluation Process*. Luria Library at Santa Barbara Community College, 2021, https://is.gd/Lc48Kk.
Charles, Leslin H., and William DeFabiis. "Closing the Transactional Distance in an Online Graduate Course through the Practice of Embedded Librarianship." *College & Research Libraries*, vol. 82, no. 3, 2021, pp. 370–88, https://doi.org/10.5860/crl.82.3.370.
Croft, James, et al. "Writing in the Disciplines and Student Pre-Professional Identity: An Exploratory Study." *Across the Disciplines*, vol. 16, no. 2, 2019, pp. 1–20, https://doi.org/10.37514/ATD-J.2019.16.2.09.
Daugman, Ellen, et al. "Designing and Implementing an Information Literacy Course in the Humanities." *Communications in Information Literacy*, vol. 5, no. 2, 2012, pp. 127–43, https://doi.org/10.15760/comminfolit.2012.5.2.108.
Diamond, Kelly. "Problem-Based Learning and Information Literacy: Revising a Technical Writing Class." *Teaching Information Literacy and Writing Studies: Volume 2, Upper-Level and Graduate Courses*, edited by Grace Veach, Purdue University Press, 2019, pp. 157–68, https://doi.org/10.2307/j.ctv15wxqwx.15.
Dinkelman, Andrea L., et al. "Using an Interdisciplinary Approach to Teach Undergraduates Communication and Information Literacy Skills." *Journal of Natural Resources and Life Sciences Education*, vol. 39, no. 1, 2010, pp. 137–44, https://doi.org/doi:10.4195/jnrlse.2010.0005u.
Edwards, Mary E., and Erik W. Black. "Contemporary Instructor-Librarian Collaboration: A Case Study of an Online Embedded Librarian Implementation." *Journal of Library & Information Services in Distance Learning*, vol. 6, no. 3–4, 2012, pp. 284–311, https://doi.org/10.1080/1533290X.2012.705690.
Engeldinger, Eugene A. "Bibliographic Instruction and Critical Thinking: The Contribution of the Annotated Bibliography." *Reference Quarterly (RQ)*, vol. 28, no. 2, 1988, pp. 95–102, https://is.gd/aaCGfa.
Faix, Allison. "Assisting Students to Identify Sources: An Investigation." *Library Review*, vol. 63, no. 8/9, 2014, pp. 624–36, https://doi.org/10.1108/LR-07-2013-0100.
Finch, Jannette L., and Renée N. Jefferson. "Designing Authentic Learning Tasks for Online Library Instruction." *The Journal of*

Academic Librarianship, vol. 39, no. 2, 2013, pp. 181–88, https://doi.org/10.1016/j.acalib.2012.10.005.

Fitzpatrick, Damian, and Tracey Costley. "Using Annotated Bibliographies to Develop Student Writing in Social Sciences." *Discipline-Specific Writing: Theory into Practice*, edited by John Flowerdew and Tracey Costley, Routledge, 2017, pp. 113–25, https://doi.org/10.4324/9781315519012.

Flaspohler, Molly R., et al. "The Annotated Bibliography and Citation Behavior: Enhancing Student Scholarship in an Undergraduate Biology Course." *CBE—Life Sciences Education*, vol. 6, no. 4, 2007, pp. 350–60, https://doi.org/10.1187/cbe.07-04-0022.

Franzen, Susan, and Colleen Bannon. "Merging Information Literacy and Evidence-Based Practice in an Undergraduate Health Sciences Curriculum Map." *Communications in Information Literacy*, vol. 10, no. 2, 2016, pp. 245–63, https://doi.org/10.15760/comminfolit.2016.10.2.26.

Gauder, Heidi, and Fred Jenkins. "Engaging Undergraduates in Discipline-Based Research." *Reference Services Review*, vol. 40, no. 2, 2012, pp. 277–94, https://doi.org/10.1108/00907321211228327.

Goodman, Xan, et al. "Applying an Information Literacy Rubric to First-Year Health Sciences Student Research Posters." *Journal of the Medical Library Association*, vol. 106, no. 1, 2018, pp. 108–12, https://doi.org/10.5195/JMLA.2018.400.

Guise, Janneka L., et al. "Evolution of a Summer Research/Writing Workshop for First-Year University Students." *New Library World*, vol. 109, no. 5/6, 2008, pp. 235–50, https://doi.org/10.1108/03074800810873588.

Hoffmann, Debra Anne, and Kristen LaBonte. "Meeting Information Literacy Outcomes: Partnering with Faculty to Create Effective Information Literacy Assessment." *Journal of Information Literacy*, vol. 6, no. 2, 2012, pp. 70–85, https://doi.org/10.11645/6.2.1615.

Hosier, Allison. "Teaching Information Literacy through 'Un-Research.'" *Communications in Information Literacy*, vol. 9, no. 2, 2015, pp. 126–35, https://doi.org/10.15760/comminfolit.2015.9.2.189.

Insua, Glenda M., et al. "In Their Own Words: Using First-Year Student Research Journals to Guide Information Literacy Instruction." *Portal: Libraries and the Academy*, vol. 18, no. 1, 2018, pp. 141–61, https://doi.org/10.1353/pla.2018.0007.

Jensen, Erin B. "Writing in the Social Sciences." *Syllabus*, vol. 6, no. 1, 2017, pp. 1–10, https://is.gd/A1Z3Or.

Jones, Leigh A. "Podcasting and Performativity: Multimodal Invention in an Advanced Writing Class." *Composition Studies*, vol. 38, no. 2, 2010, pp. 75–91, https://is.gd/bHN2aA.

Jumonville, Anne. "The Humanities in Process, Not Crisis: Information Literacy as a Means of Low-Stakes Course Innovation." *College & Research Libraries News*, vol. 75, no. 2, 2014, pp. 84–87, https://doi.org/10.5860/crln.75.2.9072.

Kalir, Jeremiah H., and Jeremy Dean. "Web Annotation as Conversation and Interruption." *Media Practice and Education*, vol. 19, no. 1, 2018, pp. 18–29, https://doi.org/10.1080/14682753.2017.1362168.

King, Jennifer. "How to Write an Annotated Bibliography." *Access*, vol. 24, no. 4, 2010, pp. 34–37.

King-O'Brien, Kelly, et al. "Reimagining Writing in History Courses." *Journal of American History*, vol. 107, no. 4, 2021, pp. 942–54, https://doi.org/10.1093/jahist/jaaa465.

Knox, Kerry J., et al. "A Positive Student Experience of Collaborative Project Work in Upper-Year Undergraduate Chemistry." *Chemistry Education Research and Practice*, vol. 20, no. 2, 2019, pp. 340–57, https://doi.org/10.1039/C8RP00251G.

Koss, Lorelei. "Writing and Information Literacy in a Cryptology First-Year Seminar." *Cryptologia*, vol. 38, no. 3, 2014, pp. 223–31, https://doi.org/10.1080/01611194.2014.915256.

Lantz, Catherine, et al. "Student Bibliographies: Charting Research Skills Over Time." *Reference Services Review*, vol. 44, no. 3, 2016, pp. 253–65, https://doi.org/10.1108/RSR-12-2015-0053.

Laskin, Miriam, and Cynthia R. Haller. "Up the Mountain without a Trail: Helping Students Use Source Networks to Find Their Way." *Information Literacy: Research and Collaboration Across Disciplines*, edited by Barbara J. D'Angelo et al., The WAC Clearinghouse / University Press of Colorado, 2017, pp. 237–56, https://doi.org/10.37514/PER-B.2016.0834.2.11.

Lau, Jesús. *Guidelines on Information Literacy for Lifelong Learning*. International Federation of Library Associations and Institutions (IFLA), 2006, https://is.gd/DW86Pn.

Leigh, Jennifer S. A., and Cynthia A. Gibbon. "Information Literacy and the Introductory Management Classroom." *Journal of Management Education*, vol. 32, no. 4, 2008, pp. 509–30, https://doi.org/10.1177/1052562908317023.

Lidzy, Sheryl. "'Doing Business In...': An Emic Training Module." *Journal of the Communication, Speech & Theatre Association of North Dakota*, vol. 23, 2010/2011, pp. 49–55.

Lowe, M. Sara, et al. "Questioning CRAAP: A Comparison of Source Evaluation Methods with First-Year Undergraduate Students." *Journal of the Scholarship of Teaching and Learning*, vol. 21, no. 3, 2021, pp. 33–48, https://doi.org/10.14434/josotl.v21i3.30744.

Luckman, Susan. "New Information Literacies: Helping University Students Critically Evaluate Information Online." *The International Journal of Learning: Annual Review*, vol. 16, no. 6, 2009, pp. 499–512, https://doi.org/10.18848/1447-9494/CGP/v16i06/46384.

Lunsford, Andrea. "Multimodal Mondays: Prezis and Source Use: Engaging in a Multimodal Annotated Bibliography." *Bits: Ideas for Teaching Composition*, 23 Mar. 2015, https://is.gd/qM1ri8.

Mackey, Thomas P., and Trudi Jacobson. "Integrating Information Literacy in Lower- and Upper-Level Courses: Developing Scalable Models for Higher Education." *The Journal of General Education*, vol. 53, no. 3, 2004, pp. 201–24, https://doi.org/10.1353/jge.2005.0006.

Martelo, Maira L. "Use of Bibliographic Systems and Concept Maps: Innovative Tools to Complete a Literature Review." *Research in the Schools*, vol. 18, no. 1, 2011, pp. 62–70, https://is.gd/el99tL.

Matthies, Brad S., and Jonathan Helmke. "Using the CRITIC Acronym to Teach Information Evaluation." *Scholarship & Professional Work*, vol. 2, 2005, pp. 65–70, https://is.gd/ceHgRH.

Mazella, David, et al. "Integrating Reading, Information Literacy, and Literary Studies Instruction in a Three-Way Collaboration." *The Learning Assistance Review (TLAR)*, vol. 16, no. 2, 2011, pp. 41–53, https://is.gd/QwUQAB.

Mills, Jenny, et al. "Beyond the Checklist Approach: A Librarian-Faculty Collaboration to Teach the BEAM Method of Source Evaluation." *Communications in Information Literacy*, vol. 15, no. 1, 2021, pp. 119–39, https://doi.org/10.15760/comminfolit.2021.15.1.7.

Mostert, Linda Ann, and Rodwell Townsend. "Embedding the Teaching of Academic Writing into Anthropology Lectures." *Innovations in Education and Teaching International*, vol. 55, no. 1, 2018, pp. 82–90, https://doi.org/10.1080/14703297.2016.1231619.

Mounce, Michael. "Teaching Information Literacy at Delta State University." *The Southeastern Librarian*, vol. 54, no. 3, 2006, pp. 35–41, https://is.gd/CXJ9Rv.

Mounce, Michael. "Teaching Information Literacy Online: One Librarian's Experience." *Delta Journal of Education*, vol. 3, no. 2, 2013, pp. 102–13.

Muñoz, Caroline Lego. "More than Just Wikipedia: Creating a Collaborative Research Library Using a Wiki." *Marketing Education Review*, vol. 22, no. 1, 2012, pp. 21–26, https://doi.org/10.2753/MER1052-8008220104.

Mussleman, Paul, and Ellen B. Buckner. "Information Literacy as a Co-Requisite to Critical Thinking: A Librarian and Educator Partnership." *The Other Culture: Science and Mathematics Education in Honors*, edited by Ellen B. Buckner and Keith Garbutt, National Collegiate Honors Council, 2012, pp. 39–52, https://is.gd/jXmJgH.

Paglia, Alison, and Annie Donahue. "Collaboration Works: Integrating Information Competencies into the Psychology Curricula." *Reference Services Review*, vol. 31, no. 4, 2003, pp. 320–28, https://doi.org/10.1108/00907320310505618.

Parkes, Mitchell, et al. "Collaborative Annotated Bibliographies: An Online Strategy to Foster Student Collaboration and Understanding." *Proceedings of EdMedia 2013--World Conference on Educational Media and Technology*, Association for the Advancement of Computing in Education (AACE), 2013, pp. 2205–11, https://is.gd/x7QUzh.

Pashaie, Billy. "Teaching Research for Academic Purposes." *The CATESOL Journal*, vol. 21, no. 1, 2010/2009, pp. 162–74, https://is.gd/o2w1Hv.

Quezada, Teresa. "Teaching the Frameworks for Writing and Information Literacy: A Case Study from the Health Sciences." *Rewired: Research-Writing Partnerships within the Frameworks*, edited by Randall McClure, Association of College and Research Libraries, 2016, pp. 189–208, https://is.gd/Sn5hQE.

Radom, Rachel, and Rachel W. Gammons. "Teaching Information Evaluation with the Five Ws: An Elementary Method, an Instructional Scaffold, and the Effect on Student Recall and Application." *Reference & User Services Quarterly*, vol. 53, no. 4, 2014, pp. 334–47, https://is.gd/X7VjrH.

Richards, Janet C. "Creating and Sharing Annotated Bibliographies: One Way to Become Familiar with Exemplary Multicultural Literature." *Reading Improvement*, vol. 52, no. 2, 2015, pp. 61–69, https://is.gd/CBPivv.

Rinto, Erin E. "Developing and Applying an Information Literacy Rubric to Student Annotated Bibliographies." *Evidence Based Library and Information Practice*, vol. 8, no. 3, 2013, pp. 5–18, https://doi.org/10.18438/B8559F.

Rinto, Erin E., and Elisa I. Cogbill-Seiders. "Library Instruction and Themed Composition Courses: An Investigation of Factors That Impact Student Learning." *The Journal of Academic Librarianship*, vol. 41, no. 1, 2015, pp. 14–20, https://doi.org/10.1016/j.acalib.2014.11.010.

Risanti, Yanidya Ulfa. "The Undergraduate Students Critical Thinking in Writing Evaluative Annotated Bibliography in Extensive Reading Class." *RETAIN: Research on English Language Teaching in Indonesia*, vol. 7, no. 1, 2019, pp. 80–89, https://is.gd/hRkUon.

Rose-Wiles, Lisa, et al. "Enhancing Information Literacy Using Bernard Lonergan's Generalized Empirical Method: A Three-Year Case Study in a First Year Biology Course." *The Journal of Academic Librarianship*, vol. 43, 2017, pp. 495–508, http://dx.doi.org/10.1016/j.acalib.2017.08.012.

Russo, Alyssa, et al. "Strategic Source Evaluation: Addressing the Container Conundrum." *Reference Services Review*, vol. 47, no. 3, 2019, pp. 294–313, https://doi.org/10.1108/RSR-04-2019-0024.

Russom, Caroline L. "First Year Research and Writing Convergences." *Academic Exchange Quarterly*, vol. 7, no. 3, 2003, pp. 194–98.

Sample, Mark. "Sharing Research and Building Knowledge through Zotero." *Learning Through Digital Media: Experiments in Technology and Pedagogy*, edited by R. Trebor Scholz, Institute for Distributed Creativity, 2011, pp. 295–303, https://is.gd/Hf43eE.

SCONUL Working Group on Information Literacy. *Seven Pillars of Information Literacy*. Society of College, National and University Libraries, 2011, https://is.gd/PbMrUT.

Sharif, Marilyn. "Re-Envisioning the Annotated Bibliography Assignment." *Innovations in Teaching & Learning Conference Proceedings Vol. 9: Learning in a Digital World*, edited by Laura Lukes, George Mason University, 2017, https://doi.org/10.13021/G8itlcp.9.2017.1834.

Spires, Hiller A., et al. "Going Global with Project-Based Inquiry: Cosmopolitan Literacies in Practice." *Journal of Adolescent & Adult Literacy*, vol. 63, no. 1, 2019, pp. 51–64, https://doi.org/10.1002/jaal.947.

Stadler, Derek. *Writing Effective Annotated Bibliographies Using Blackboard's Discussion Board*. CUNY LaGuardia Community College, 2018, https://is.gd/Ylry7P.

Sternadel, Lisa. "Inquiry and Developing Interpretations from Evidence." *The Science Teacher*, vol. 71, no. 4, 2004, pp. 38–41, https://is.gd/AGCA1j.

Tan-de Ramos, Jennifer. "Effects of Teaching Strategies in Annotated Bibliography Writing." *Journal of Education and Practice*, vol. 6, no. 7, 2015, pp. 54–57, https://is.gd/uFU4KD.

Whatley, Kara. "Making Instruction Audience-Appropriate: Information Literacy for Non-Traditional Students." *Brick and Click Libraries: An Academic Library Symposium*, edited by Frank Baudino et al., Northwest Missouri State University, 2006, pp. 100–04, https://is.gd/IqX8kh.

Winicki, Barbara Ann. "Reading Teachers and Research: From Consumers to Evaluators to Producers." *Journal of Reading Education*, vol. 31, no. 2, 2006, pp. 21–28.

Winslow, Rachel Rains, et al. "Not Just for Citations: Assessing Zotero While Reassessing Research." *Information Literacy: Research and Collaboration Across Disciplines*, edited by Barbara J. D'Angelo et al., The WAC Clearinghouse / University Press of Colorado, 2017, pp. 287–304, https://doi.org/10.37514/PER-B.2016.0834.2.14.

Zanin-Yost, Alessia. "Academic Collaborations: Linking the Role of the Liaison/Embedded Librarian to Teaching and Learning." *College & Undergraduate Libraries*, vol. 25, no. 2, 2018, pp. 150–63, https://doi.org/10.1080/10691316.2018.1455548.

6 Library Support

Luke Beatty

Introduction

This chapter discusses strategies librarians can use to support annotated bibliographies (ABs) outside of credit-bearing instructional contexts. Because there is virtually no peer-reviewed scholarship on this topic, most of the advice in this chapter comes from my experience working with ABs in traditional library settings/contexts. To this end, I recommend five ways that librarians can support ABs outside their credit-bearing classrooms:

- Single-session support.
- Reference desk work.
- Production of educational materials.
- Faculty liaison and outreach.
- Collaboration with campus offices.

Single-Session Support

Librarians will often be invited into classes to help students prepare for upcoming AB assignments. If you find yourself so invited, here are a few things you can do to prepare for your session:

- Get a copy of the syllabus and the AB assignment before class. Ensure you understand how the class is structured and what the AB assignment requires students to do.
- Get in touch with the instructor *before* the session. A short phone call, email, or in-person chat will do. Get a fulsome understanding of what the instructor wants from you. Should you focus on formatting? Writing different types of annotations? Citing sources? Will you need more than one session?
- Get a realistic sense of the students you will be working with. Is this a first-year remedial writing course? Is it a

fourth-year capstone? What must the students know in order to succeed?
- Propose spreading your visits out over a few classes (for a shorter time) rather than a single visit (for a longer time). This gives students more opportunities to familiarize themselves with you, is less taxing on their attention spans, and allows them to check in with you at various stages of their assignment. Because instructors do not have to sacrifice a whole class, a surprising number of them will opt for several shorter visits.
- Once you have your marching orders, plan liberally. Ensure your materials have clear writing, are aesthetically pleasing, and display your contact information prominently. Prepare to do some legwork if the instructor has not introduced the assignment or forewarned the class of your visit(s). If you need to brush up on ABs, see "Chapter #3: Teaching Annotation Types," "Chapter #5: Librarian Assignments" and "Chapter #9: Three Sample Annotated Bibliographies." As the class winds down, remember to let students know that you are there to help. Be explicit about the kinds of AB help you provide, including the following:
- Help with formulating research questions.
- Help with finding sources.
- Help with AB formatting (in *Word*, *Google Doc*s, or *Pages*).
- Help with citing sources, including bibliography checking via email or at the reference desk.
- Help with writing and/or editing annotations.
- These assurances can have a real impact on the volume of students who seek follow-up appointments!

Reference Desk Work

For libraries still staffing a reference service – either physically or digitally – my guess is that you get a steady stream of AB questions. None of the AB questions you get should stretch you too much, but a little preparation can help you at the desk. Here are some low-effort initiatives to ease your work at the desk when handling AB questions:

- Ensure you have laminated copies of your library's citation guides – preferably the latest versions of APA, MLA, and Chicago styles – at the ready. If your library has not produced its own guides, find some to use from another library. Also,

- if your desk has space, keep a laminated sample AB for quick sharing. For those working on a digital reference desk, ensure it has shareable copies of your library's citation guides and sample ABs.
- Ask students to show you their AB assignments. You want to ensure you understand the instructor's expectations. Your base assumption should be that students will have at least one curveball in their AB assignments. Instructors will sometimes require discipline-specific formats, describe ABs and annotations idiosyncratically, or otherwise require non-standard AB variants.
- Have a firm command of how to format documents in *Word* and *Google Docs*, paying special attention to the formatting functions needed for ABs (e.g., indentation, special spacing, hard and soft returns). Students will want help formatting their ABs, and 95% of the time they will be using *Word* or *Google Docs*. With *Google Docs*, be mindful that some functions that are easy to perform in *Word* are significantly more complex in, or absent from, *Google Docs*.
- If your reference desk does not yet have mirrored dual monitors, talk to someone about getting that set up. Dual monitors will significantly improve your reference work by facilitating a more fluid collaboration between you and the student. Absolutely essential for face-to-face operations.

One last note for supporting ABs at the reference desk: be prepared for the occasional student who has lost composure. I have seen students frustrated, exhausted, and even in tears over their AB assignments. Librarians who have worked at a reference desk before will have evolved strategies for dealing with these high-tension encounters, so dig into your sympathy bag and be ready to put in some work.

Production of Educational Materials

While single-session support is a fantastic way to help students with their ABs, making key resources available in the library and online can be just as important. With no prior knowledge of ABs, students could use the following resources to help them with their assignments:

- Citation guides and citation generators. Most students begin their ABs by citing sources, so having a good set of citation

guides and links to the best (free) citation generators should be a priority. If your library is unable to produce in-house guides, consider linking to a reliable set elsewhere (see https://library.ic.edu/cite for examples).
- A basic guide to writing ABs. This guide should include information about what an AB is and examples of how to write it.
- A sample AB, preferably downloadable in *Word* format. Over the years, a number of students have thanked me for making an AB template available to them. Consider taking an afternoon to write an AB yourself as students get a kick out of seeing a familiar name on the materials they use.
- Ensure students can easily discover these resources on your library's homepage with minimal clicking. Regardless of where you house these resources, though, ensure your faculty are aware of them and be prepared to link to them when building course guides, handouts, and so forth. If possible, try to get your links listed on as many learning management systems sites as you can. The more places a link appears, the greater chance students will find it.

Faculty Liaison and Outreach

Working directly with students on their assignments is the gold standard of library support, but working directly with instructors on their *assignment design* pays dividends as well. Getting instructors to invite you into their assignment design process is no easy feat, but with some initiative and a healthy working relationship you can make it happen. Here are three liaison and outreach strategies I have found to be particularly useful:

- The not-so-cold email. In the summer, I gather up syllabi from all the courses taught at my college in the previous year. I then map out the assignments listed in those syllabi. For AB outreach, I identify those instructors who assigned ABs and then send them an email offering library support via class visits, customized educational material, and/or assignment design assistance. Instructors typically treat these outreach efforts warmly.
- The "librarian-certified" program. One service you might extend to faculty involves an arrangement whereby students must consult a librarian before submitting their AB assignments. In doing this, the librarian helps students avoid crummy

sources, bad formatting, and failure to adhere to assignment instructions. While labor-intensive, the "librarian-certified" program can make you indispensable to faculty.
- Assignment design micro-workshops. One way to motivate faculty participation in co-designing assignments is with a little money. Talk to your library administration about freeing up money for micro-workshops – half a day or a couple of hours – in which you and one instructor sit down and design an AB assignment together. Prepare a package of pre-existing AB assignments and high-impact design practices, and make those available to the instructor before the workshop. Keep your workshop short and have some fun. Before you know it, you will be collaborating with many instructors on a number of different assignments.
- Assignment design group workshops. If time is short and money is tight, try brown-bag group that utilize some of the practices outlined above.
- In the interests of working smarter before working harder, consider these strategies. Catching problems at the design stage will benefit both students and instructors alike, and when it comes to AB assignments, no one is better positioned to catch problems than you.

Collaboration with Other Campus Offices

While the library should develop strong relationships with faculty, cultivating strong relationships with other campus offices is also important. In terms of supporting AB assignments, the campus writing center and academic coaches are the library's most vital student-support partners. To bolster chances for student success, ensure the library, writing center, and academic coaches are comfortable with the following:

- Picking up the phone and talking with one another. Know one another's names, know who does what, and make time to keep abreast of changes in your respective areas. Students needing help with AB assignments could end up in either the library, the writing center, or an academic coach's office, and knowing where to direct students is crucial.
- Working with a common set of resources. Students should get a consistent message when seeking AB help, and the library, writing center, and academic coaches should work from a common

set of materials. In the interests of reducing headaches, let librarians take the lead in designing these materials, but to get more buy-in, collaborate with interested parties.
- Training student workers to make appropriate referrals. As anyone who has spent time on campus will recognize, students learn as much from their peers as they do from academic professionals. Ensure your student workers know where to send their peers for help. A good referral can be the difference between getting excellent assistance and getting no assistance at all. A simple cheat sheet for your student workers can be a life-saver: "If students have question x, send them to... if students have question y, send them to..."

Students might also conceivably seek AB help from elsewhere on campus. Ensure these offices know that the library provides AB help. For athletes, team coaches commonly make referrals; mental health counselors can be in the mix; speech centers frequently field questions; and I am sure countless other offices do as well. Basically, keep your ears to the ground and talk to people outside your immediate circle. You never know when a relationship can help a student. By the same token, know the library's limits, and do not be afraid to make referrals to the campus writing center or academic coaches when students are working on their ABs.

7 Writing Center and Academic Coaching Support

Cynthia A. Cochran

Introduction

Helping students compile annotated bibliographies (ABs) is one of the most crucial ways to support them in their research writing process. By writing an AB – which is an organized list of citations and notes about their sources – writers can use the AB as a way to think through their research plans. That is why the assignment is so common in higher education: from first-year composition through graduate-level courses in every discipline, students are asked to compile ABs. Whereas students can get AB assistance from librarians, your advice as an academic coach or a writing center consultant can be crucial.

Depending on how much research the student has done, you can provide valuable assistance at almost every stage of the AB writing process. Of course, students who ask for your help *before* selecting a topic or locating sources may best be referred to their instructor or a librarian. Assuming students have found their sources but have yet to read them, writing center consultants would not normally be required to help them do so. At this stage, however, coaches in language centers and other academic support offices may become involved. Typically, though, students will seek your help after they have already found sources, taken notes, or even drafted their AB.

Beginning the Support Session

A little background: some ABs are standalone "papers," but most are a step toward a complete research paper. A preliminary AB is a very early step in research and is usually quite short. A complete AB is longer and is typically the last step before the student drafts a research paper or research proposal. For graduate students, the

AB precedes the dissertation, master's thesis, or sometimes a bibliographic essay.

The first step in helping students with an AB is to prepare for your session:

- Consider the experience of the student. Ask whether this is the student's first AB and what kind of help or feedback they need.
- Ask to see the assignment and check requirements carefully to ensure that you and the student understand any special instructions regarding length, format, documentation style, and expectations for annotations.
- Check the syllabus or ask the student about the timeline of the project, especially to see if it is a standalone product or part of a larger assignment sequence. If the student is going to use the sources to write a paper, for example, that may well affect the type and depth of annotations needed.
- Consider the student's stage in the writing process. For example, if the assignment is for a preliminary AB, short annotations are generally acceptable. Ask if the student will be revising the preliminary AB later into a complete AB.
- Likewise, consider the course for which the AB is being written, including the course level and discipline. Each discipline has its own genre conventions for research writing. These include documentation style, organization, and even the type of annotations expected. Some examples of differences across courses:

    ○ Most ABs are alphabetized, but ABs for history are often organized chronologically. Check the assignment.
    ○ Some courses focus on research methods. Do annotations mention the methods used in the sources?
    ○ Although ABs are typically written in complete sentences, in some fields, annotations may be written with bulleted lists/sentence fragments. This is true, for example, in business or science writing, where lists are common.

Checking Annotated Bibliography Format

Formatting an AB is dependent upon the instructor's criteria, but some features are fairly common. Here is an example of how an AB should be formatted in MLA.

[Header starting on page 2]

[Student Name]
[Professor Name]
[Course Name and Number]
[Date]

Annotated Bibliography: [My Topic]

Prefatory remarks with thesis, followed by source entries and annotations. Entries are alphabetically organized by author surname, unless otherwise specified by instructor.

Anagram, Annie. *An Extremely Long Book about Extremely Unimportant Things: A Treatise.* Scholarly Publishing, Inc., 2022.

The first annotation immediately follows the first citation. The paragraph is flush left -- usually in line with the indented part of the citation -- and has as many sentences as needed. Most annotations are one paragraph long, but they can contain as many paragraphs as needed. Put one blank line after this paragraph and before the next citation.

Blogger, Bob. *Boring Things You Will Never Need to Know: Burgers & Their Makers.* Aardvark Hill Press, 2020.

The second annotation follows immediately after the second citation. Again, the paragraph is flush left in line with the indented part of the citation, and the paragraph has as many sentences as necessary. Annotations of different types can be part of the same paragraph. See "Chapter #3: Teaching Annotation Types" for more details.

Clogger, Carla. *Fifty Methods of Catching Rattlesnakes: A Manual for Beginners.* Prairie Rattler Press, 2015.

The third annotation follows immediately after the third citation. The paragraphs are flush left in line with the indented part of the citation.

If there is a second paragraph, add one blank line after the first paragraph. The second paragraph should be indented in the same way as the first paragraph.

Introductory Paragraphs

An AB typically has an introductory paragraph stating the topic/problem, the research question(s), and a working thesis statement. In some cases, instructors may also wish students to include a statement about the scope of the research, meaning the parameters within which the research project will be performed. For example, in an AB for a history course, the AB's introduction paragraph(s) might mention the type of materials being sought (e.g., primary sources from a given era).

Some students, especially at the advanced undergraduate or graduate levels, may be working on lengthy ABs for theses and dissertations. Because they are attempting to gain a foothold on all the relevant research they can locate, they may also need to write more elaborate AB introductions. Such introductions typically mention issues such as the scope of their research. They may also mention the importance of the research topic and identify a prospective audience for the AB.

Annotation Entries

The bulk of the AB consists of individual entries, each with a bibliographic citation followed by the annotation paragraph(s). Instructors may specify the format and organization of AB entries. If the instructor has not done so, you can use the following guidelines:

- Citations should follow the documentation style used in or appropriate to the course (for further guidance, see the Checking Documentation Style section below).
- Most citation styles use hanging indent paragraph format and look just as they would in the Works Cited, References, or Bibliography of a research paper.
- Each annotation appears below its source citation, with one blank line intervening. There is also a blank line after the annotation paragraph but before the next source citation.
- Annotations and citations may be single-spaced or double-spaced, depending on the instructions or relevant style.
- Annotation paragraphs typically are in block format, with the left margin lining up with the indented part of the citation or the left margin of the page.
- Annotations are typically written with complete sentences, though for some purposes they may reasonably include lists or sentence fragments.

- Annotation entries are typically organized alphabetically. However, in some cases, the instructor or the nature of the research project may call for the organization to be chronological, topical, or divided by other categories. Within these categories, entries may be alphabetized.

Concluding Paragraphs

Most ABs do not have or need a conclusion. Some do. Concluding paragraphs should be double-spaced or single-spaced, just as the introduction. Longer ABs may require lengthy conclusions of several paragraphs. Concluding paragraphs in ABs recap the writer's most important findings. Some also identify gaps in the research, perhaps making suggestions for further study.

Checking Documentation Format

Format needs to adhere to the documentation style used in the class. Check documentation styles by consulting a style manual, reliable citation generator, or library guide (see https://library.ic.edu/cite for examples). Be prepared to locate information on less common documentation styles. Most assignments, however, require documentation in the APA 7, MLA 9, or Chicago 17 styles. Although these styles share many attributes, first-year students may have trouble. Other students will encounter problems if they have previously used one style and now must adapt to another. This is not the only formatting problem you will encounter. For example, students may need reminders to place the citation *before* the annotation. As another example, students may not realize they need to use hanging indentation for citations and block indentation for annotations. Here is a listing of the prominent features of the APA 7, MLA 9, and Chicago 17 styles.

Feature	APA 7	MLA 9	Chicago 17
Commonly Used by...	Natural, social, and physical sciences	Arts & humanities	History, art history, religion, editing and publishing, and philosophy
Pagination/ Running Head	Title, writer surname, and page number at top of page	Writer's surname and page number ½ inch from top of page, starting on page 2	Writer's surname (optional) and page number starting on the top of page 2
Format of Title (centered)	Annotated Bibliography: The Topic	Annotated Bibliography: The Topic	Annotated Bibliography: The Topic
In-text citations (if any)	(Author, year, page if quoting), e.g., (Johnson, 2019, p. 33)	(Author page), e.g., (Johnson 33)	(Author year, page if quoting) e.g., (Jones 2019, 33)
Title of source list in Bibliographic Essay or Research Paper	References	Works Cited	Bibliography OR References
Author names in Works Cited or References	Smith, A.S. OR Smith, A.S., & Bone, L.L.	Smith, Ann S. OR Smith, Ann S., and Leo L. Bone	Smith, Ann S. OR Smith, Ann S. and Leo L. Bone
Order of References, Bibliography, or Works Cited	Alphabetized by author, then chronological from earliest to most recent for authors with multiple works	Alphabetized by author, then alphabetical by title of work for authors with multiple works	Alphabetized by author, then alphabetized by title of work for authors of multiple works

If a student needs more help with citations beyond being directed to a documentation guide, you might want to overview some of the most important features of citations. Of course, citation elements vary from one source type to another (e.g., book chapters list different information than do journal articles). Here is a listing of common citation features in the APA 7, MLA 9, and Chicago 17 styles, in order of their appearance in the citation.

APA 7	*MLA 9*	*Chicago Style 17*
• Creators and contributors (initials and surname, not given names) • Publication date • Title • Version, volume, and issue number, if any • Page numbers • Publisher • Virtual location, if applicable (URL or DOI, database if no URL or DOI)	• Creators and other contributors (full names) • Title of source and its container(s) • Version, volume, and issue numbers, if any • Publisher • Publication date • Database name, if any • Virtual location, if applicable (URL or DOI)	• Creators and other contributors (full names) • Title • Version, volume, and issue numbers, if any • City of publication • Publisher • Publication date • Virtual location, if applicable (database, URL or DOI)

Helping with Annotations

Of course, you will devote the bulk of your tutoring session to reviewing the student's annotations. Usually, you will neither see nor have time to read the sources being annotated, so your goal should be to treat the annotations as you would any text, by considering the writing quality. Using some simple guidelines will make your approach more efficient and effective. First, check how well the annotations correspond to the AB instructions and purpose. Also, check how well the writer has used one or more of the five types of annotations:

- Descriptive annotation – Identifies the main features and/or sections of a source.
- Summative annotation – Recaps the main points and/or arguments of a source.
- Evaluative annotation – Judges the credibility, reliability, and/or value of a source.
- Reflective annotation – Indicates how a source may be used in one's work or the field.
- Combined annotation – Incorporates two or more of the aforementioned annotation types.

Be aware that instructors may use alternative vocabulary when describing annotations, so be prepared to do some on-the-fly translation. One prominent variation you will see is that some instructors will ask for a "critical" annotation, which usually corresponds to an evaluative or a combined annotation type in our parlance. The key to remember is that the AB serves to record research in an organized way and, usually, to prepare one for writing a research paper. These purposes are served by the five annotation types.

Using the checklist below, assess the quality of the annotations as you talk to the writer. Remember that annotations vary, and that the writer may not need to exhaustively comment on every single source. This checklist will help you and the writer focus on the content of the annotations if you use it to guide your questions.

CHECKLIST: Things to Consider for a Complete Combined Annotation

- How detailed does the description need to be (given a reader who has no access to the work)?
    - Does it identify the author and source format?
    - Does it mention whether the source is popular, scholarly, or peer-reviewed?
    - Does the writer need to further describe the source?
- To what degree does the writer adequately summarize the source?
    - Besides the main thesis and purpose (which should be included no matter what), does the writer need to add crucial supporting points or detail?
    - For argumentative sources, does the writer adequately convey the main line of reasoning?
    - Are there any crucial facts, definitions, or quotes the writer wants to include?
- To what extent does the writer evaluate the source?
    - Is there something important about the author or publisher that affects the work's credibility?
    - Does the writer need to consider the content, argument, or conclusion?
    - Does the writer evaluate the extent that the methods are appropriate to the subject and carried out well?
- Does the writer reflect upon the utility of the source for writing a paper?
    - How and/or where might the writer use it in the paper?
    - If it is a "bad" or "mediocre" source, is there a good way to use it?
    - Has the writer reflected on how the source relates to other sources cited?
- Do any annotations need to go into more depth given the source and the topic?
- See "Chapter #3: Teaching Annotation Types" for additional annotation checklists.

Significant Problems to Consider

Writers may need some assistance with the different annotation types:

- Regarding descriptive annotations, writers may not have correctly identified the source type, authorship, or key sections of a work. They also may have trouble figuring out whether a source is peer-reviewed, or even whether it is popular or scholarly.
- Student summaries may be shallow, which is perfectly fine for a preliminary AB (whose purpose is merely to get a start on choosing sources for a research project), but may be inadequate for a complete AB. If you notice a very short summary of a very long text, ask the writer whether there is more content that should be included.
- Novice writers, especially, tend to write list-like summative annotations. Whereas this tendency is appropriate for summarizing some informational texts and scientific studies, it is not a good way to summarize arguments. If you think this is a problem, talk to the writer about using transitions that help convey a line of reasoning.
- When evaluating the quality of a source, student writers may not know what to say about its credibility, especially if they are first-year writers. Help them look up author bios, ask them about author credentials, talk about the publication date, identify the source type, fact-check major claims, and so on. Critiquing the source is ultimately the student's responsibility, but you can help.
- In the early stages of research, it is difficult for some writers to reflect on how and where to use a source in their paper, so talking through their reflective annotations can inspire them.

More broadly speaking, some writers rely on quotes in their annotations. Typically, one does not quote in an annotation, but if warranted, students should include a page number of the quoted passage. Another major problem is the unethical use of the source text or abstract. In no case should students use any part of an abstract instead of their own wording when composing an annotation. If you notice sudden changes in the formality and vocabulary of the AB, talk to the writer about plagiarism.

One final note: it can be difficult to coach or consult writers working in fields that are very different from your own, especially when students are using conventions that are special to their disciplines. In other chapters in this volume, you will see plenty of examples of citations, annotations, and ABs in APA 7, MLA 9, and Chicago 17 styles. The key is to treat the AB like any other writing assignment: focus on the writer's developing awareness of how an AB can be a satisfying and crucial step in their research experience.

8 Teaching Source Types

Luke Beatty and Cynthia A. Cochran

Introduction

Students use a variety of source types when writing their annotated bibliographies (ABs), and this chapter discusses some of the problems they encounter working with those sources. These problems can impact the quality of both their annotations and their citations. For each source type, we outline problems that students may encounter, and we offer practice-based advice for addressing these problems. (In many cases, however, simply alerting students to a given problem may be all you need to do.) Though this list is by no means exhaustive, in our experience it covers the majority of source types that student researchers typically use:

- Books
- Book Chapters
- Academic Journal Articles
- Magazine Articles
- Newspaper Articles
- Encyclopedia Articles
- Websites and Webpages
- Blogs, Podcasts, and Social Media
- Audiovisual Material
- Government Publications and Technical Reports
- Images and Art
- Dissertations and Theses
- Videogames
- Literary Works

Though some advice in this chapter might strike veteran faculty as commonplace, we have routinely seen undergraduates – particularly in their first and second years – struggle to identify, cite, and annotate particular source types. Our advice accordingly tries to get into the headspace of undergraduates and identify why/how these sources cause them trouble. We hope our advice and observations will help your students write their ABs more effectively.

Books

Books are common and well-regarded research sources, but we have seen students have problems working with them. The usual obstacles apply – difficulty navigating library catalogs, picking an appropriate title, finding the time to read carefully, or even refusing to use books because "I don't need to use more than five pages." But we have also encountered more surprising dilemmas, such as students' inability to even identify books as such or differentiate between fiction and non-fiction books. Here are some roadblocks we have seen when students annotate books:

- Recognizing that online books and e-books are actually books. Some students mistake e-books for long articles, reports, or other non-book sources. Take some time to explain e-books.
- Differentiating academic from popular books. Students often believe that all books held in academic libraries are scholarly, and this belief can lead them to some very questionable research findings.
- Establishing the reputability of a book publisher. We have seen any number of self-published and vanity books included in student ABs. If this is a problem, consider providing a list of reputable publishers in your syllabus to help minimize student difficulty.
- Failing to select relevant sections/chapters of a book to annotate, or inadequately summarizing anything other than the introduction of a book. Five minutes of instruction will help.
- Regarding literary works, parsimoniously summarizing a plot is difficult for many students. If this is a requirement for your AB assignment, devote time to plot summaries in class or in your materials.

Book Chapters/Book Sections

When students annotate book chapters or sections, they encounter many of the same difficulties they have with annotating books.

Book chapters/sections have unique challenges, however, and students often stumble on the following:

- Producing a reasonable citation for a book chapter in an edited volume. Even beyond struggling with the mechanics of producing a citation, many students cannot identify either a book's editor or a chapter/section's author. Take some time to teach students the differences between editors and authors.
- Correctly identifying a book chapter as such. Students often mistake book chapters for journal articles, and this is especially true when chapters are accessed via databases or online platforms.
- Misunderstanding a book chapter's relationship with the book itself. Taking ideas out of context is a fixture of early-undergraduate research, and taking book chapters in isolation can exacerbate student tendencies toward overgeneralization.
- Failing to notice other relevant chapters after finding a chapter they want to use. Conversely, sometimes students get sidetracked on irrelevant or extraneous chapters.

Academic Journal Articles

Academic journal articles are some of the most commonly used sources in undergraduate research, but they are also some of the trickiest to annotate. Without overgeneralizing, we note that professors in the hard sciences typically ask for descriptive and summative annotations, while professors in the humanities often prioritize evaluative and reflective annotations. It may be helpful to familiarize your students with disciplinary- and class-specific expectations before having them annotate academic journal articles. Here are some struggles we see when students use academic journal articles:

- Failing to differentiate between academic journal articles and popular magazines articles. A single-session visit by a librarian can be helpful in nipping this issue in the bud.
- Identifying a journal title, volume/issue, publication date, and page numbers. Train your students to access PDF copies of articles when available, as bibliographic information is often contained on the first page of the article. HTML or web versions of the same article do not always display this information (or sometimes even have it at all).

- Reading, understanding, and engaging with academic writing.
- Skimming through important sections of the article and failing to deep-read. This is a leading cause of students' inability to effectively annotate an article. A quick search will reveal a wealth of professional literature on how to help students read academic journal articles.
- Reading only the abstract/precis/summary of the article.
- Failing to distinguish arguments from counter-arguments, such as those that may appear in a literature review or discussion section of the article.
- While there are no quick fixes for many of students' reading problems, they can be directed to academic support offices and reading coaches (if your campus has them).

Encyclopedia Articles

Undergraduate students love using encyclopedia articles. We have found students gravitate toward encyclopedia articles when (a) they need an effective summary of an issue, (b) when they have difficulties working with peer-reviewed literature, or (c) when a specialized encyclopedia is an appropriate resource. (Which is not to call these bad habits, merely to note them.) With that as background, we have observed the following difficulties with encyclopedia use:

- The encyclopedia article can be conflated with an academic journal article, especially if the student found it through a database or online forum.
- Students are occasionally unaware that they need to cite encyclopedia articles. They believe that encyclopedic information is sufficiently well-known and established, and as such does not require citation. In some cases, this may be true, but in most cases it is not.
- As with book chapters, students have difficulty differentiating encyclopedia article authors from encyclopedia editors. A sit-down with a librarian can help them figure this out.
- Students who use encyclopedias may not recognize the utility of the references therein. Point that out! With wiki or wiki-like encyclopedias, students can be easily encouraged to follow the links.
- Because encyclopedia articles contain background and foundational information, they lend themselves well to descriptive and summative annotations. Let students know this.

- Similarly, because encyclopedia articles are well-vetted, an evaluative annotation is typically unnecessary beyond noting the encyclopedia's trustworthiness.

Magazine Articles

In a recent library class, Luke asked his students what magazines they would expect to find in their dentist's office. One student deadpanned, "I just look at my phone." Despite a lack of print magazines in their environment, students still find a variety of magazine articles when they search online and in databases. However, they might not realize that what they have found are magazine articles. Instructors would do well to offer students guidance on this matter. Here are some issues our students encounter with magazine articles:

- Students may be unaware of the differences between popular magazine and academic journals. Let students know it is OK to ask their instructor, librarian, coach, or writing center consultant for help.
- Citing online versions of magazine articles, without page numbers, can get tricky for students. They should be directed to use PDF versions of articles when possible.
- When students write evaluative annotations of a magazine article, they tend to focus on the article's style and aesthetics rather than the article's substance. In most courses, they should not do this (with art, media studies, and communications courses being some notable exceptions).
- Students will often notice the more opinionated/ideological nature of magazine articles. Encourage students to remark upon this in their evaluative annotations.

Newspaper Articles

As with magazines, students are finding fewer and fewer physical newspapers in their environment. The online newspaper/news site is flourishing, however, and students continue to use a variety of news articles in their research. Here are some recurrent issues we encounter when students work with news articles:

- Citing online news articles can be tricky. Take a moment to review where students might find key information in a news article, such as publication date, author, and article title.

- While students typically consume their news online, they are not necessarily attuned to the differences in quality among news sources. A library session geared toward source evaluation can help students better select and evaluate news articles.
- Differentiating between news reporting, editorials, book reviews, and feature columns can be difficult for novice researchers. Some discussion of these elements might be in order. (Students should be advised to avoid using book reviews as research sources other than in literary studies.)
- Easy access to international news sources is wonderful, but sometimes students inappropriately select international sources. For example, a student researching welfare in the US might select a news article discussing welfare in India instead of an article discussing welfare in the US. For obvious reasons, this is a problem.
- We recommend summative and reflective annotations be used when students annotate news articles from reputable news outlets. While evaluative annotations are of course always welcome, they are especially crucial in annotations of investigative reports, exposés, longer features, or news from less-than-reputable sources.

Websites and Webpages

As instructors know, many students do not select the most reliable and trustworthy online sources. This is of course symptomatic of a larger information literacy deficit in a world already rife with (dis/mis)information, but one should at least take a few moments to discuss online source selection. Here are some observations from our practice about how students use and approach websites and webpages:

- Novice researchers may fail to distinguish between a webpage (a single page or document on a website) and a website (a collection of webpages). A good analogy to tell your students is that if the website were a house, the webpages would be rooms in the house.
- Domain extensions – such as.EDU or.GOV – are reasonably good indicators of the type and quality of information one can expect from a given website. Students respond well when taught what key domain extensions mean.

- Finding publication dates on websites can be tricky. Have students look at the top or bottom of the page, and possibly even in the URL, if all else fails. Luke's rule: no date, no cite.
- Website authorship can be equally tricky to establish. You can advise students to use publisher names if they cannot locate an author.

Blogs, Podcasts, and Social Media

Students are increasingly using blogs, podcasts, and social media in their research. Because there are no uniform guidelines regarding the quality and transparency of these resources, instructors need to take special care in helping students work with them. We tend to emphasize the following points in our instruction:

- The authorship of social media is often anonymous or ascribed to a username, but there will usually be a time and date to govern citations. Ensure that students note this information.
- Students may underestimate the time it takes to annotate un-transcribed podcasts, and instructors may find it difficult to verify the accuracy of the student's annotation in any meaningful way.
- Owing to the personal and idiosyncratic nature of social media, postings can give an excellent anthropological snapshot of a culture or society. Ensure your students provide a context to convey the significance of these sources.
- Because of the uneven quality of blogs and podcasts, students should take care to evaluate the worth/value of these sources.
- Influencers, advocacy groups, and commercial interests can effectively disguise themselves online. The evaluative annotation is an effective tool for helping students identify and responsibly use these sources.

Audiovisual Material

Contemporary students use multimodal sources in their research. This trend is driven not only by the accessibility of audiovisual (A/V) material on streaming sites, but also by assignments allowing students to find A/V material. Unfortunately, A/V sources are not always easy to use in the research process. Consider:

- We notice that some developmental writers rely on A/V materials, because they are afraid to engage with textual sources. This is obviously a multi-faceted problem, but be aware that it happens in the source-selection process.
- Remind students that A/V materials can be found outside their immediate social media bubble or usual streaming services. Campus streaming services such as *Kanopy* or *Swank* are great places to search.
- Producing A/V citations is notoriously complex. Consider using library or writing center help if you expect your students to have problems.
- Annotation can be time-consuming with un-transcribed A/V material. Let students know that transcriptions may be available for podcasts, videos, and other A/V materials.
- In the halcyon days of yore, students skipped the book and watched the video. Nowadays, they skip the video and read the plot summary! Unfortunately, students may not cite these plot summaries. Such is life. Direct them to a plagiarism checker.

Government Publications and Technical Reports

Government publications and technical reports are foundational materials in certain fields. Students in those fields will periodically work with these sources. Government publications and technical reports are notoriously difficult to cite, so be aware that students may need assistance working with them. Here are some tips to help your students:

- Identifying the proper department, office, or agency producing these publications can be tricky. Citation generators can help, but if the publication is in PDF format the students will have to locate this information themselves.
- Government and academic reports are generally well-researched, so an evaluative annotation may be unnecessary beyond noting the trustworthiness, bi-partisanship, or timeliness of the report.
- Occasionally, however, reports produced by advocacy groups or undemocratic governments provide misleading information. Teaching students how to evaluate this information is a winning strategy.

Images and Art

As the Internet has made images and artworks easily accessible, students have increasingly incorporated them in their research. We have really enjoyed seeing the creative ways students use these materials, though there are some trouble spots you can help your students avoid:

- Citing online images or artworks using just a URL is common. Some instructors will allow this practice in less formal contexts – like a PowerPoint presentation or a class handout – but formal written work requires that students properly cite all sources.
- Forgetting to note the creation date of images is a problem. Finding such a date is not always easy, so be charitable in grading citations.
- Including reproductions of images and artwork in ABs can be useful. However, students may forget to adequately describe these works, but a picture is not worth 1,000 words! Advise students to write their descriptive annotations as if their reader has no access to the image or artwork in question.
- Regarding images-which-aren't-art (e.g., charts, graphs, or infographics), chances are the image (or its data) conveys some form of argument. Have students write a summative annotation to get the gist of the data or to capture the essence of the argument.

Dissertations and Theses

Because dissertations and theses are now widely available online, students have used them more frequently in recent years. Though graduate students and academic professionals are still the primary audience for dissertations and theses, master's theses are popular with undergraduate students owing to their constricted length. We offer the following tips for your students when they work with dissertations and theses:

- Your institution's masters and doctoral dissertations may be available through an institutional repository.
- The literature review and bibliography within a dissertation or thesis may help students find additional sources. In doctoral dissertations, these sections are typically comprehensive.

- As doctoral dissertations are dense and jargon-laden, students can have trouble distilling the information they find into a useable annotation. To minimize confusion, students should focus only on chapters they need.
- Dissertations will frequently find new life as articles, book chapters, or even books. If available, these materials may be easier for your students to read. Tell students to search for work by the dissertation/thesis author, which can lead them to materials that are easier to annotate.

Videogames

As videogames are now the go-to form of entertainment for college students, it is unsurprising they want to use them in their research. Unlike other sources discussed in this chapter, videogames feature a user-directed experience – rather than an author-directed experience – because they have an infinite number of stories and play possibilities. This makes them difficult to annotate. With that as background, here are tips for students who work with videogames:

- As games are updated frequently, citing a particular game iteration can be challenging or effectively impossible. Best advice: have students look for a version number (if applicable).
- Students may assume a familiarity with their videogames that may not be shared by all. Remind students that descriptive and summative annotations should impart context.
- As with other narrative forms, students are prone to over- or under-describe plot. When annotating, students should write for a reader who is new to the game.
- Though videogames are primary source documents, we have seen students inappropriately cite historical (mis)information from videogames. Reminding students that, say, Assassin's Creed: Odyssey is not an authoritative source on Greek history is now an unfortunately necessary caveat.
- When students' research newly released videogames, they might not find immediately relevant scholarly material. This lack of scholarship can frustrate students when it conflicts with their assignment instructions (especially when they are forced to use only peer-reviewed journal articles). Evaluative and reflective annotations can help students justify their use of popular sources when scholarly material does not yet exist.

Literary Works

Students who research literary topics will probably work with both primary source documents (the literature itself) and secondary materials (works discussing the literature). Annotating literary works is an art unto itself, and should you find yourself working with students who need to annotate primary source literature and secondary material, consider the following:

- Students may opt to use secondary sources to help them summarize fiction works. Remind students that doing this is acceptable and formally citing their secondary sources is mandatory.
- Annotating literary works requires students to mention elements other than plot – such as style, tone, literary era, and so on – yet many students neglect to discuss these elements in their annotations.
- Novice writers may over-summarize plot and under-utilize secondary materials. Encourage the use of secondary materials where appropriate.
- Literary scholarship can be dense and jargon-heavy, and this can predictably cause problems with annotations. Suggest close reading and frequent breaks.
- Students may wish to work with fan fiction, but they may have difficulty evaluating the quality of these works. Have students consider the qualities that make the source literature distinctive, and then have them evaluate the degree to which the fan fiction mirrors those qualities.

9 Three Sample Annotated Bibliographies

Luke Beatty and Cynthia A. Cochran

Introduction

In this chapter, we provide three sample annotated bibliographies (ABs) in the APA 7, MLA 9, and Chicago 17 (Notes and Bibliography) styles. Each AB addresses a different topic and is written in a style consistent with a competent undergraduate student's work. These samples are useful for explaining the form and purpose of ABs to students. In the AB, we endeavor to capture the variety of source types that students actually use in their research (e.g., journal articles, books, websites). For guidance on teaching students how to annotate different source types, see "Chapter #8: Teaching Source Types." Most of the sample annotations in this chapter are of the combined type (being some mix of descriptive, summative, evaluative, and/or reflective annotation types). For purposes of demonstration, however, the annotations in these sample ABs are somewhat condensed. For further guidance on teaching annotation types, see "Chapter #3: Teaching Annotation Types." Feel free to use these sample ABs for non-commercial, educational use.

Sample APA 7 Annotated Bibliography

Math anxiety and dyscalculia are common problems. My research paper will be about how middle school and secondary school students cope with these disabilities. My working thesis is that a variety of coping strategies can successfully combat math anxiety, and I hope to find many examples supporting this in my literature search. In my paper, I will discuss the prominent strategies I discover to combat math anxiety, and I will also discuss how these strategies can be adapted to help racialized and minoritized students (who are often particularly afflicted with math anxiety and/or dyscalculia).

Ashcraft, M. H. (2019). Models of math anxiety. In I. C. Mammarella, S. Caviola, & A. Dowker (Eds.), *Mathematics anxiety: What is known and what is still to be understood* (pp. 1–19). Routledge.

This book chapter, by Ashcraft, provides research-based summaries of the predominant models used to describe math anxiety. This chapter offers excellent material to ground my research, and while I have not yet decided which theory/model of math anxiety I find most convincing, I will devote an initial section of my paper to recapping the models Ashcraft identifies.

In this chapter, Ashcraft summarizes the personality construct model (math anxiety derives from aspects of an individual's personality); the cognitive construct model (math anxiety is thought to occupy space in an individual's working memory); the sociocultural construct model (teachers, parents, curricula, etc., are thought to influence math anxiety); the gender model (math anxiety is somewhat determined by sex/gender differences); the neuro-biological model (math anxiety is somewhat determined by genetic factors); and the interpretation model (math anxiety partly derives from an individual's *perception* of why they struggle with math).

Association for Psychological Science. (2015, November 4). *Math anxiety doesn't equal poor math performance*. https://is.gd/AXzyzO

This Association for Psychological Science article discusses a study in which the authors examine the relationships between math anxiety, math performance, and math motivation in US college students. The findings of the study were surprising: those with modest math anxiety and high math motivation saw an increase in their math performance over time; conversely, those with a small degree of math anxiety and a low level of math motivation saw a decrease in their math performance.

This research is significant because it suggests that interventions to reduce math anxiety may not always be productive or advisable, especially if the anxiety is modest and the motivation is high. To date, in my research, this is the only source pointing out a "positive" side to math anxiety, and so this source is valuable. Since I will argue for specific interventions to reduce math anxiety, I will refer to this source in discussing the potential costs of said intervention.

Doedens-Plant, A. C. R. (2018). *An investigation into the associations between maths anxiety in secondary school pupils and teachers' and parents' implicit theories of intelligence and failure* [Doctoral Dissertation, University of Southampton]. https://is.gd/ihm1mp

This doctoral dissertation, by Doedens-Plant, " . . . examined the role that teachers' mindsets, or implicit beliefs about intelligence and failure, play in the development of their pupils' mindsets and subsequent maths anxiety" (p. "abstract"). An empirical survey in Britain of 859 secondary-school students, 84 parents, and 9 teachers asked about their beliefs about intelligence and failure in relation to math anxiety. The study revealed that students and teachers' beliefs about failure impacted students' math anxiety. The study concludes that math teachers can help reduce math anxiety by promoting failure as a helpful part of learning. Insofar as I could determine, the study's methodology was sound, and the author's conclusions follow from the evidence.

Kranzler, J. H. (2018). *Statistics for the terrified* (6th edition). Rowman & Littlefield.

Statistics for the Terrified addresses math anxiety that accompanies statistical learning. Statistics are obviously a subset of mathematics, and I would like to devote a section of my paper to difficulties learning statistics. Though I will cite information from the entire book, the three chapters in Section #1 are the most useful for me: "Effective Strategies for Studying Statistics"; "Overcoming Math Anxiety"; and "Basic Math Concepts." In these chapters, Kranzler argues that rational emotive therapy – a type of psychotherapy – can help overcome math anxieties. Rational emotive therapy aims to conquer feelings that (a) are unpleasant and (b) lead to self-defeating behaviors. I have not seen this therapy discussed in my other research, but it struck me as quite useful, so I will use this source in my statistics anxiety section.

Shaffer, L. (2015). The fear of math: Five strategies to help students conquer their math anxiety. *Scholastic Instructor, 124*(5), 27–29.

This magazine article, by Shaffer, reviews five strategies used by elementary school teachers to reduce math anxiety. These strategies are (1) to promote a growth mindset; (2) to begin each lesson with a comforting warm-up activity; (3) to allow multiple pathways to an answer; (4) to not let the desire for speed become a roadblock; and (5) to make math a game. Though the evidence backing these strategies is anecdotal, and this is not a peer-reviewed journal article, the suggestions make sense and probably would work. Most of these strategies also incorporate a social/partnering dimension, which other sources recommend for combatting math anxiety.

Young, J. R., & Young, J. L. (2016). Young, black, and anxious: Describing the black student mathematics anxiety research using confidence intervals. *Journal of Urban Mathematics Education, 9*(1), 79–93. https://is.gd/5M30Ir

This meta-analysis, published in a peer-reviewed journal, aims to "... conduct a single group summary of studies using the [Math Anxiety Reporting Scale] to characterize and delineate the measurement of reported [math anxiety] within the Black Student population" (p. 83). In their meta-analysis, the authors analyze 21 studies of K-12 populations that included black students. Regretfully, they could not find enough evidence about black students and math anxiety to draw firm conclusions. The authors' lack of findings suggests an urgent need for more studies devoted to black students and math anxiety, and I plan to discuss this in my paper. I will also look for sources about other underrepresented populations and math anxiety.

Sample MLA 9 Annotated Bibliography

I consider comic books and graphic novels to be literature. Although only a few comic books and graphic novels are treated with any seriousness in literary discussions, I will make the case that comic books and graphic novels should be considered literature. In my research for this annotated bibliography, I would like to learn more about the distinctions between fiction and literature, and I want to investigate the history of why comic books and graphic novels have been ignored by critics until recently. As an education major, I am also interested in how comic books and graphic novels are used in the classroom, so some of my research will focus on teaching with those materials.

Cleaver, Samantha. "Comics & Graphic Novels." *Instructor*, vol. 117, no. 6, 2008, pp. 28–34, https://is.gd/Y2zeOM.

Samantha Cleaver's short magazine article highlights pedagogical reasons why comic books and graphic novels are taught in elementary classrooms. In addition to readily connecting with students, comic books help strengthen students' visual and multimodal literacies. Though the article is brief, it reinforces the fact that comic books and graphic novels are now taught alongside conventional children's literature. I found at that many teachers rely on *Instructor* magazine, so I trust the source. Using this and other sources, I will make a populist argument that as elementary students graduate into high school and college, they will bring their assumptions about the literary value of comics with them.

Emina, Seb. "In France, Comic Books Are Serious Business." *The New York Times*, 29 Jan. 2019, https://is.gd/KKGEUd.

This newspaper article, by Seb Emina, reports on France's annual *Angoulême International Comics Festival*. The author notes that by sales volume, most comics and graphic novels in the French/Belgian market are selling better than ever. Experts quoted in the article also suggest that the quality of these publications is higher than ever. This scene contrasts with the American market, where comic book and graphic novel sales tapered off as of 2018. Some information from this article will be useful as background/contextual material in my research, but I will also look for more updated figures.

Liu, Jonathan H. "Comics as Literature, Part 1: The Usual Suspects."
WIRED, 1 June 2012, https://is.gd/AOAaTA.

This web article, by Jonathan Liu, lists a selection of comic books and graphic novels he considers literary. Liu is more fan than scholar, but his writing is well-informed. He discusses *Watchmen* (by Alan Moore), *Sandman* (by Neil Gaiman), *Maus* (by Art Spiegelman), and *Understanding Comics* (by Scott McCloud). Aside from providing useful summaries of these comic books, Liu's judgment about their literary merit stands as a model of populist insight into what "Joe Shmoe" considers literary.

McCloud, Scott. *Understanding Comics: The Invisible Art*. Harper Perennial, 1994, https://is.gd/s4yfXn.

This graphic novel, by Scott McCloud, is a foundational work in comic book and graphic novel studies. *Understanding Comics* makes a book-length argument about what comics are and how they evolved. A good deal of my research thus far has mentioned this graphic novel, and it is a great resource for definitions and key concepts in the comics world.

Understanding Comics has become an ingrained part of the conversation about comic books and graphic novels, so I knew I had to read it. The chapters I plan to cite are "The Vocabulary of Comics" (great for definitions); "Time Frames" (explaining how the passage of time is conveyed with panels); and "Show and Tell" (discussing how pictures and words came to intermingle, and why people view that combination as less intellectually demanding than words alone).

Petersen, Robert S. "The Return of Graphic Narratives for Adults." *Comics, Manga, and Graphic Novels: A History of Graphic Narratives*, Praeger, 2011, pp. 205–226, https://is.gd/JegDAw.

This book chapter, by Robert Peterson, surveys the adult-and-alternative comics movements of the 1960s–1990s. In arguing that comic books are literature, I would like to discuss the 1960s' alternative comics movement in the US and the contemporaneous *bandes dessinées* style in France. This chapter discusses some of key publications in these respective movements.

Though many alternative comics and *bandes dessinées* were "adult" in the sense that they dabbled in erotica, many also spoke to controversial political and social themes. Addressing such themes marked these publications as more "literary" than mainstream comics of the day.

Spry, Adam. "Louis Riel: A Comic-Strip Biography." *Critical Survey of Graphic Novels: Independents and Underground Classics.*, edited by Bart Beaty and Stephen Weiner, 2nd ed., vol. 2, Salem Press, 2019, pp. 487–90.

This encyclopedia entry, by Adam Spry, summarizes and critiques the graphic novel *Louis Riel*, first published in 2003. The entry contains six sections: "Publication History," "Plot," "Characters," "Artistic Style," "Themes," and "Impact." Capturing the essence of a graphic novel is difficult, and I like how Spry has broken down *Louis Riel*, so that is one of the reasons I will use this source.

Another reason I will use this source is to make a strong case that *Louis Riel* shares two important similarities with most literary works. First, the author, Chester Brown, was responsible for every aspect of the graphic novel (writing, art, inking, lettering, drawing panel borders, etc.), which makes him very much like the sole author of a novel. Second, every page of *Louis Riel* features a layout of two columns and three rows, and this constancy mirrors the unvarying page-by-page arrangement of literary prose.

Stripped. Directed by Dave Kellett & Frederick Schroeder, Sequential Films, 2014, Apple TV, https://is.gd/YOQuGL.

This documentary film, by Dave Kellett and Frederick Schroeder, features several prominent cartoonists discussing the artistry, cultural impact, and business of comic strips. Besides being a great background source, this film also demonstrates that the pressures involved in publishing a daily newspaper forced comic strips to evolve differently from their comic book cousins. The comic-strip-as-literature argument is not central to my paper, but I will use this source to note that comic strips are even lower on the literary totem pole than comic books and graphic novels. I hope to find a suitable print resource to supplement this video.

Sample Chicago 17 (Notes and Bibliography) Annotated Bibliography

I am writing a research paper about capital punishment in America. My personal belief is that the death penalty is rarely warranted, but I will limit my paper to the argument that capital punishment in America has been unfair and racist. My research will attempt to contextualize contemporary cases of the death penalty against the historical record, showing that racism and inequities have persisted throughout the history of capital punishment in America.

Abili, Emily Jean. 2013. "A Historical Comparative Analysis of Executions in the United States from 1608 to 2009." Doctoral Dissertation, Las Vegas, NV: University of Nevada, Las Vegas. https://is.gd/LdftTQ

As per Abili, this doctoral dissertation "... examines the history of executions, including lynchings, in the United States from 1608–2009..." (2). In order to write the historical background of my paper, I plan to use the chapters "Early America (1608–1815)" and "The Long Nineteenth Century (1789–1920)." Though other works address capital punishment in early America, Abili's thesis is unique because it chronicles not only legal but also extra-judicial killings. This is the only source I have found on extra-judicial killings. The other chapters in the dissertation do not interest me. Since this is a dissertation, I think it is trustworthy.

Aratani, Lauren. 2018. "Capital Punishment in the US Continues Decline Despite Slight Rise in 2018." *The Guardian*, December 14, 2018, sec. World news. https://is.gd/7Lsz70

This newspaper article, by Lauren Aratani, reports on the long-term decline of execution rates and capital convictions in the US. Aratani notes that since 1995, when public fears about criminality were peaking, executions and capital trials decreased. Aratani also notes that the decline would have been sharper were it not for Texas and Florida, who accounted for more than half of current US executions at that time.

The article also cites an opinion poll showing that the US public is evenly split (+/−5%) on whether there should be a death penalty and whether it is applied fairly and impartially. I will use some facts and figures from this article in my paper, and since *The Guardian* is an established and reputable newspaper, I have faith in the information.

Aviv, Rachel. 2015. "Revenge Killing: Race and the Death Penalty in a Louisiana Parish." *The New Yorker*, July 6, 2015. https://is.gd/xRV64P

In this magazine article, Rachel Aviv tells the story of Rodricus Crawford, a young man from Caddo Parish, Louisiana. Crawford was convicted – falsely, it would seem – of murdering his infant son. Caddo Parish is the most prolific county in the US for issuing death sentences, and Aviv blames systemic racism, biased policing, and an unstable prosecutor as the reasons for this circumstance. The reporting is powerful, and Aviv balances observations about capital punishment in the US with the particulars of Crawford's case. I have chosen this article, because it provides me with a contemporary example and because it offers insights on the arbitrariness of the death penalty.

Brunello, Anthony R. 2016. "Politics, Ethics and Capital Punishment in America." *Review of History and Political Science* 4 (1): 13–30. https://is.gd/0h2B1l

This article, by Anthony Brunello, examines capital punishment in America. Brunello demonstrates that the death penalty, as currently practiced, is (1) neither swift nor sure; (2) neither fair nor equitable; (3) cost ineffective; and (4) not in line with global practices. He also chronicles the 1972–1976 US moratorium on the death penalty. Though many sources discuss this period, Brunello's treatment is readable. The cases here really interest me, so I might consult newspapers from the 1972–1976 moratorium to learn more.

Congressional Research Service. 2016. *Federal Capital Offenses: An Abridged Overview of Substantive and Procedural Law*. Congressional Research Service. https://is.gd/kk9dNL

This report, authored by the Congressional Research Service, provides constitutional and legal information pertaining to capital punishment in America. The report has three sections: "Introduction," "Constitutional Considerations," and

"Existing Federal Law." The introductory section contains a wealth of basic information, while the latter section includes a comprehensive discussion of death-eligible offenses. As the Congressional Research Service is bipartisan and apparently trustworthy, and the report is recent, I plan to use it in my paper. This is the most succinct, fact-based source I have yet found.

Lyon, Andrea D. 2015. "The Death Penalty Yesterday and Today." In *The Death Penalty: What's Keeping It Alive*, 1–21. Rowman & Littlefield.

Andrea Lyon's book chapter relates a history of the death penalty in America from 1607 to 2015. The chapter highlights landmark decisions, philosophical considerations, and procedural issues related to capital punishment. As a history, this chapter provides a readable overview of the death penalty in America. As a critique of the death penalty, the chapter highlights post-conviction acquittals, differing standards of evidence, cost-(in)effectiveness of the death penalty, and other issues. Lyon's analysis will help me write the background section of my paper and may provide some arguments for my analysis.

Mandery, Evan J. 2013. *A Wild Justice: The Death and Resurrection of Capital Punishment in America*. New York: W. W. Norton & Company.

This book, by Evan Mandery, explores the 1972 Supreme Court decision *Furman v. Georgia*, in which the Supreme Court ruled that capital punishment violated the Eighth Amendment's prohibition against cruel and unusual punishment. As a fiction writer, Mandery has written a fast-paced and engaging book describing the justices, caselaw, and political climate of the time. This book provides a wonderful account of *Furman v. Georgia* and the ensuing four-year moratorium on capital punishment. To close the book, Mandery covers the 1976 case *Gregg v. Georgia*, which ushered in the return of the death penalty. This is the most thorough resource I have found on why the death penalty was struck down (and subsequently overturned), and so I will definitely use it.

Glossary

abstract a written summary of a work's context, purpose, key points/arguments, problem, research questions, thesis/ hypothesis, methods, findings, and conclusions. Also called *précis* (in business) or *synopsis* (in art, culture studies, and film).
annotate the act of taking notes on a text or other artifact.
annotated bibliography an organized list of citations wherein each citation is annotated; typically alphabetized, though entries may be arranged chronologically, topically, geographically, and so on.
annotation a note about a source; can be **descriptive, summative, evaluative, reflective,** or **combined**.
bibliographic citation information identifying source texts, appearing in a reference list, including, e.g., author, publisher, page numbers, and publication/creation date.
bibliographic essay a specialized literature review summarizing and organizing research, and including bibliographic information in a continuous prose narrative.
bibliography an organized list of citations, most often alphabetized, including entries identifying information needed to locate the listed sources. In APA-style papers, called **References**; in MLA-style papers, called **Works Cited**; in Chicago-style papers, called **Bibliography** or **References**.
Bibliography the name for a list of references in the Chicago style, as well as some other styles.
citation a written identifier of a source, appearing in either a footnote, endnote, in-text parenthetical reference, or bibliography. (See **reference**.)
combined annotation a note using at least two of the descriptive, summative, evaluative, and reflective annotation types.

Glossary

descriptive annotation a note about the nature of a source, typically listing features such as creators, topic, composition, publication format, and other pertinent details.

Digital Object Identifier (DOI) a unique code made of numbers, letters, and symbols used to permanently identify and link to an online document.

documentation style set of guidelines for citing sources; formatting guidelines for bibliographies and other research-based writing. Many styles are associated with particular disciplines and professions. Also called *citation style* or *reference style*.

endnote a citation appearing at the end of a paper, chapter, or book. (See **footnote, in-text citation**)

evaluative annotation a note judging credibility, reliability, logic, and/or value of a source, as well as the credibility of a source's authors/creators.

footnote a citation appearing at the bottom of a page. (See **endnote, in-text citation**.)

in-text citation a reference to a source in the body of a text. Also called a *parenthetical reference*. (See **footnotes, endnotes**.)

literature review a narrative summary and appraisal of scholarship on a given topic; may include all or only the most important or relevant scholarship.

permalink a permanent and unchanging link to an online source.

preliminary annotated bibliography a simplified version of an annotated bibliography. May include only brief descriptive annotations; some include reflective and/or evaluative annotations.

reference another word for *citation*; a written identifier of a source, in either a footnote, endnote, in-text citation, or bibliography. (See **citation**.)

References the name of a bibliography in the APA and (sometimes) Chicago styles.

reflective annotation a note telling where and how one might use a source in one's research.

summative annotation a note recapping a source's main points, argument(s), or plot.

Works Cited title of a bibliography in the MLA and (sometimes) Chicago styles. Also used in some other documentation styles.

Index

Note: **Bold** page numbers refer to tables.

abstract 153, 158
abstract/precis/synopses 158, 176
academic AB author 4
academic coaching support 144; annotated bibliography format 145–6; annotation entries 147–8; concluding paragraphs 148; documentation format 148–50; helping with annotations 150–2; introductory paragraphs 147; support session 144–5
academic journal articles 157–8
academic librarians 13–14
academic sources **106**
academic support 144, 158
academic vocabulary 153
accessibility 45
Agosti, Maristella 2
allied health fields 17–18
alphabetical order 4
alternative vocabulary 151
American market 25
American Psychological Association (APA) 3, 166–9
annotated bibliography (AB) 4–5; annotated bibliography 73–4; annotations 1–2; argumentative essay 73–4; assignment sheet 96–8; bibliographic essay 5, 81–2; bibliographies 3–4; citations 2–3; collaborative annotated bibliography 88–9; complete annotated bibliography 64–5; credit-bearing classrooms 138;
definition of 1–2; format 145–6; in higher education 9–23; history of 1–6; reference desk work 139–40; related forms 5; related forms online 5–6; requirements for 56–7; writing process 144
annotating literary works 165
annotation quality **106**; basic annotation skills **51**; group annotated bibliography **125**; scaffolded annotated bibliography **130**; simplest annotated bibliography **101**; *see also* annotation writing quality
annotations 1–2; definition of 1–2; elements in combined annotations **76**; entries 147–8; format 145–6; history of 1–2
annotation types 24–5, 153–4; combined annotation 38–40; descriptive annotations 26–8; evaluative annotation 32–7; summative annotation 28–31
annotation writing quality: annotated bibliography **75**, **83**; argumentative essay **75**; basic annotation skills **51**; complete annotated bibliography **66**; preliminary annotated bibliography **58**
APA *see* American Psychological Association (APA)
APA 7 annotated bibliography 166–9

Index

APA Publication Manual 3
argumentative essay: activity description 70; assumptions 74; audience 69, 74; instructions 72–3; learning outcomes 69–70; overview 73; rubric 75–6; teaching notes 70–2; timeline 69; variants 72
artworks/online images 163
assignment design 44; common elements 95–6; process of 141
assignment sheet, common elements 96–8
Association for Psychological Science 167
audiovisual (A/V) material 161–2
authorship, social media 161

Balsamo, Luigi 3, 4
basic annotation skills: activity description 46–7; assignment 49–50; assumptions 50; audience 46, 50; instructions 49–50; learning outcomes 46; overview 49; rubric **51–2**; teaching notes 47–8; timeline 46; variants 48–9
bibliographic citation 46, 53, 147
bibliographic essay 5; activity description 78; audience 77, 82; collaborative writing 49, 89; instructions 81; learning outcomes 77; overview 81; requirements for 82; rubric **83–4**; teaching notes 78–80; timeline 77; variants 80
bibliographic information 3, 157
bibliographies 3–4; alphabetical order 4; annotated bibliography 24; chronological order 4; definition of 96; ecclesiastical texts 4; list of sources 49, 56; preliminary 56; subject bibliography 5
blogs 161
book chapters/sections 156–7
books 156
born-digital objects 5

Catholic Church, religious scholarship 4

checklist: combined annotation 39–40; descriptive annotation 27–8; evaluative annotation 34; summative annotation 31
Chernin, Eli 2
Chicago 17 173–5
The Chicago Manual of Style 3
chronological order 4
citation, format of, history of 2–3
citation management tools 5
citations 2–3; AB and essay **84**; annotated bibliography **75**; argumentative essay **75**; basic annotation skills **52**; combined annotations **112**; common elements 94–5; complete annotated bibliography **67**; concepts of 60, 69; different source types, AB with **106**; group annotated bibliography **125**; library's citation guides 139–40; management tools 5; plug-and-play, generation service 44, 96; preliminary annotated bibliography **58**; scaffolded annotated bibliography **130**; simplest annotated bibliography **101**
citation styles 2–3, 98, 147; *see also* documentation styles
cognitive construct model 167
Colaianne, A. J. 4
collaboration: campus offices 142–3; instructor-librarian 11–14
collaborative annotated bibliography: activity description 86; assumptions 90; audience 85, 90; instructions 88; learning outcomes 85; overview 88; rubric 90; teaching notes 86–8; timeline 85; variants 88
collaborative writing, assignments for 49, 86, 89
combined annotations: baseline assignment sheet changes 109; checklist 39–40; MLA 9 style 39; outcomes 108; standards alignment **109**; suggested rubric **111–12**; teaching notes 110
comics and graphic novels 25
common documentation 3
community 32

complete annotated bibliography: activity description 61; assignment 64; assumptions 65; audience 60, 65; checklist 152; instructions 64; learning outcomes 60–1; overview 64; rubric **65–8**; teaching notes 61–3; timeline 60; variants 63
complex full-cite 2
composition 42; AB assignments for 42; argumentative components 69; bibliographic essay assignment 77; research component of 85; WAC courses 53
composition courses 42, 77; advanced composition courses 77; assignments for 42–90; developmental composition courses 42; *see also* writing across the curriculum (WAC) classes; writing courses
comprehensive literature reviews 158, 163
conclusion **84**, 148
Congressional Research Service 174
Connors, Robert J. 2
content management systems 5
coping strategies 166
Council of Writing Programs **43**
creativity 32
creators 29, 32, 35
credibility, judging 25, 32, 62, 151
credit-bearing classrooms 138
"critical" annotation 151
critical annotations *see* evaluative annotations; reflective annotations
critiques *see* evaluative annotations

descriptive annotation quality: basic annotation skills **51**; complete annotated bibliography **67**; preliminary annotated bibliography **58**
descriptive annotations 153; checklist 27–8; MLA 9 style 26–7; quality **51, 59, 66**
descriptive sentence 38
descriptive & summative annotation elements **111**

different source types, annotated bibliography: baseline assignment sheet changes 104; outcomes 103; standards alignment **104**; suggested rubric **106**; teaching notes 104–5
digital archives, online archive collections 1, 5
digital humanities 5
Digital Object Identifier (DOI) 3, 150, 177
Diigo Web Collector 5
dissertations and theses 163–4
documentation format 148–50
documentation styles 78, 145, 147, 148; *see also* citation styles
documentation system 44
Dombrowski, Quinn 5
domain extensions 160
double-spaced lines 147, 148
Drupal 5

e-books 156
ecclesiastical texts 4
educational materials 140–1
ELA *see* English Language Arts (ELA)
elementary school teachers 169
encyclopedia articles 158–9
endnotes 3, 177
engagement 125
English Language Arts (ELA) **43**
English-language vocabulary 4
evaluative annotation 32–7; checklist 34; elements **111**; MLA 9 style 32–3; quality, complete annotated bibliography **67**; reflective annotation 35–7
Evernote 5
exchange information 2

faculty liaison and outreach 141–2
Ferro, Nicola 2
fiction books 156
Fihrist al-'Ulum 4
first-year writing course 14–15
footnotes 2–3, 177
format/formatting 29, 32, 35; AB and essay **84**; annotated bibliography **75**; argumentative essay **75**; basic annotation skills

52; combined annotations **112**; common elements 95; complete annotated bibliography **68**; different source types, AB with **106**; group annotated bibliography **125**; preliminary annotated bibliography **58**; scaffolded annotated bibliography **130**; simplest annotated bibliography **101**
French/Belgian market 25

Galen (physician) 3
Garcia, Antero 2
gender model 167
general education course 14–15
Gibbon, Edward 2
Google Docs 5, 55, 62, 72, 95, 97, 140
Google Sheets 63, 88, 118–20
government publications 162
graduate level courses 144
group annotated bibliography: baseline assignment sheet changes 123–4; outcomes 122; standards alignment **123**; suggested rubric **125**; teaching notes 124
group workshops 142

handwritten manuscripts 1
hanging paragraph formats 120, 147
hard sciences 17–18
Harvard style 2
helping with annotations 150–2
higher education: academic librarians 10, 13–14; academic professionals 10; allied health fields 17–18; annotated bibliography 9–23; assess student learning 19–20; bibliographers 10; first-year writing course 14–15; general education course 14–15; humanities 15–16; learning assessment tools 20–1; librarian-instructor collaborations 11–13; manuals and skill books 10–11; mathematics 17–18; online learning 21–2; scaffolding tools 18–19; social sciences 15–16; student-facing books 10

The History of the Decline and Fall of the Roman Empire (Gibbon) 2
humanities 3, 5, 15–16, 157

IL *see* information literacy (IL)
images and art 163
indentation 95, 120, 140, 148
information literacy (IL) courses 44, 93; assignments for 19–20; common elements 93; *see also* library courses
Internet 163
in-text citations 3, **149**
introductory paragraph: AB and essay **83**; annotated bibliography **75**; argumentative essay **75**; basic annotation skills **51**; complete annotated bibliography **66**; group annotated bibliography **125**; preliminary annotated bibliography **58**; scaffolded annotated bibliography **130**; simplest annotated bibliography **101**
introductory paragraphs 147

Journal of Research in the Teaching of English 4
judgments, making *see* evaluative annotations

Kalir, Remi 2
Krummel, Donald William 3, 4, 5

learning assessment tools 20–1
legal citation styles 98, 100, 104, 109, 115, 119, 173
length of an annotated bibliography 10, 47, 148
letter-and-number systems 2
LibGuides 9
librarian 44
"librarian-certified" program 141
librarian-instructor collaborations 11–13
library: administration 142; of Alexandria 3; campus offices 142; catalog/databases 64, 73, 139; ecclesiastical texts 4; instruction 46; subject bibliography 5

library courses, assignments for 159, 160; *see also* information literacy (IL) courses
Library of Harvard's Museum of Comparative Zoology system 2
library support: collaboration, campus offices 142–3; educational materials 140–1; faculty liaison and outreach 141–2; reference desk work 139–40; single-session support 138–9
line spacing 40, 48, 62, 63, 73, 146, 147, 174
literary scholarship 165
literary works 165
literature review 38, 158, 163

magazine articles 159
manuals and skill books 10–11
marginalia 1
Mark, Edward Laurens 2
mathematics 17–18
Microsoft Excel 63, 88, 118–20
Microsoft Word 5, 55, 62, 72, 140
micro-workshops 142
MLA *see* Modern Languages Association (MLA)
MLA Handbook 3
MLA 9 style: annotated bibliography 170–2; combined annotation 39; descriptive annotation 26–7; evaluative annotation 32–3; reflective annotation 35–6; summative annotation 29–30
MLA Style Sheet 3
Modern Languages Association (MLA) 3
Muhammad ibn Abi Ya'qub Ishaq al-Nadim 4

National Council of Teachers of English **43**
newspaper articles 159–60
Nielsen, Danielle 45
non-fiction books 156
notes 1, 44, 45, 144, 173
not-so-cold email 141
novice researchers 160
novice writers 153, 165

Omeka 5
online annotated bibliography 5–6, 21–3
online archival collection 5
online books 156
online citation generators 44, 47, 54, 62, 140, 148
online learning 21–2
online sources 160
online tools 5
ordering: alphabetical order 4; chronological order 4; subject bibliography 5
organizational modes 118
organization and coherence **84**
outline, using the annotated bibliography to create 74, 78, 90

paraphrasing 48
permalink 118, 120
personality construct model 167
Pinakes 3
plagiarism 47, 48, 55, 63, 72, 153, 162
planning 70, 78, 85, 86
plug-and-play citation generation service 44
podcasts 161
popular sources **106**
PowerNotes 5
preliminary annotated bibliography: activity description 53–4; assignment 56; assumptions 57; audience 53, 57; instructions 56–7; learning outcomes 53; overview 56; rubric **58–9**; teaching notes 54–5; timeline 53; variants 55–6
primary source documents 165
printing press 1, 3, 4
publication dates 161
Publication Manual of the American Psychological Association 3
publication of annotated bibliographies 162

quotations 31

readability 32

184   Index

reference desk work 139–40
references 24, 94, 147, 158; *see also* citations
reflective annotation: checklist 37; complete annotated bibliography 67; elements 112; MLA 9 style 35–6; quality 67; scaffolded annotated bibliography 130
religious scholarship 4
research papers 14, 18, 48, 49, 53, 56, 61, 64, 77, 85–90, 127, 173
rhetorical purposes 47, 50, 57, 65, 74, 82, 90
rough draft, using the annotated bibliography as 71, 87, 90
rubrics **51–2, 65–8,** 75–6, **83–4,** 90, **111–12, 125, 130**

scaffolded annotated bibliography: baseline assignment sheet changes 128; outcomes 127; standards alignment **128**; suggested rubric **130**; teaching notes 129
scaffolding tools 18–19
scholarship, in-text citations 3
secondary materials 165
shared documents 86, 87
simplest annotated bibliography: baseline assignment sheet changes 100; outcomes 99–100; suggested rubric 101; teaching notes 100–1
single-session support 138–9
social annotation 21–2
social media 161; idiosyncratic nature 161
social sciences 3, 15–16
source: author(s) and format 38; features 118; format 4; knowledge of 35; unethical use of 153; variety of **106, 125**; *see also* source quality
source evaluation annotated bibliography: baseline assignment sheet changes 115; outcomes 114–15; standards alignment 115; suggested rubric **116–17**; teaching notes 116
source quality **58, 66, 75**; AB and essay **83**; annotated bibliography

75; argumentative essay **75**; combined annotations **112**; complete annotated bibliography **66**; preliminary annotated bibliography **58**; scaffolded annotated bibliography **130**; simplest annotated bibliography **101**
source-selection process 162
subject bibliographies 5
summative annotation: checklist 31; MLA 9 style 29–30
summative annotation quality **52, 66**; basic annotation skills **52**; complete annotated bibliography **67**

teaching, notes 47–8, 54–5, 61–3, 70–2, 78–80, 86–8, 100–1, 104–5, 110, 116, 120, 124, 129
teaching source types: academic journal articles 157–8; audiovisual material 161–2; blogs, podcasts, and social media 161; book chapters/sections 156–7; books 156; dissertations and theses 163–4; encyclopedia articles 158–9; government publications 162; images and art 163; literary works 165; magazine articles 159; newspaper articles 159–60; technical reports 162; videogames 164; websites and webpages 160–1
technical reports 162
titles 2
Tribble, Evelyn B. 2

UD *see* universal design (UD)
universal design (UD) 45
University of Chicago (Chicago) 3
US Geological Service 2
US Government Printing Office 2

videogames 164
visual annotated bibliography: baseline assignment sheet changes 119–20; outcomes 118–19; standards alignment **119**; suggested rubric **120–1**; teaching notes 120

website authorship 161
websites/webpage annotations 160–1
Wellisch, Hans H. 4
working thesis statement 147
Works Cited/Bibliography/References lists 147
World Bibliography of Bibliographies (Besterman) 4
write annotations 45
writing about writing 88
writing across the curriculum (WAC) classes: argumentative essay 69–76; basic annotation skills 46–52; bibliographic essay 77–84; collaborative annotated bibliography 85–90; complete annotated bibliography 60–8; preliminary annotated bibliography 53–9; standards alignment **43**
writing across the curriculum/writing in the disciplines, assignments for 46–90
writing center, writing center support 142–54
writing courses, assignments for 14–15, 138; *see also* composition courses
writing quality 150

Zotero 5–6

For Product Safety Concerns and Information please contact our EU representative GPSR@taylorandfrancis.com
Taylor & Francis Verlag GmbH, Kaufingerstraße 24, 80331 München, Germany

www.ingramcontent.com/pod-product-compliance
Lightning Source LLC
Chambersburg PA
CBHW051741230426
43670CB00012B/2108